Grandma's Comfort Food—Made Healthy

ALSO BY JOANNA M. LUND

The Healthy Exchanges Cookbook
HELP: The Healthy Exchanges Lifetime Plan
Cooking Healthy with a Man in Mind
Cooking Healthy with Kids in Mind
The Diabetic's Healthy Exchanges Cookbook
The Strong Bones Healthy Exchanges Cookbook
The Best of Healthy Exchanges Food Newsletter '92 Cookbook
Notes of Encouragement
It's Not a Diet, It's a Way of Life (audiotape)

Grandma's Comfort Food–Made Healthy

A HEALTHY EXCHANGES® COOKBOOK

JoAnna M. Lund

HELPing Others HELP Themselves
the **Healthy Exchanges® Way™**

A Perigee Book

A Perigee Book
Published by The Berkley Publishing Group
A member of Penguin Putnam Inc.
200 Madison Avenue
New York, NY 10016

For more information about Healthy Exchanges products, contact:
Healthy Exchanges, Inc.
P.O. Box 124
DeWitt, Iowa 52742-0124
(319) 659-8234

Perigee Special Sales edition: January 1998
ISBN: 0-399-52427-4
Published simultaneously in Canada.

The Putnam Berkley World Wide Web site address is
http://www.berkley.com

Printed in the United States of America

10 9 8 7 6 5 4 3 2 1

Before using the recipes and advice in this book, consult your physician or health-care provider to be sure they are appropriate for you. The information in this book is not intended to take the place of any medical advice. It reflects the author's experiences, studies, research, and opinions regarding a healthy lifestyle. All material included in this publication is believed to be accurate. The publisher assumes no responsibility for any health, welfare, or subsequent damage that might be incurred from use of these materials.

This cookbook is dedicated to the entire QVC "family," from the book buyers to the on-air hosts, from the production staff to the hardworking order representatives answering the phones, and of course to the viewers at home. Each has embraced this middle-aged grandma from the cornfields of Iowa and brought her into that wonderful fellowship called QVC.

Contents

Acknowledgments

I'm so thankful to QVC for helping me spread the word to all of you about my "common folk" healthy recipes and commonsense approach to healthy living. But without the complete support of so many, I couldn't do what I do. For doing "whatever needs to be done" and doing it quickly, I want to thank:

John Duff and Barbara O'Shea from Putnam and Paula Piercy and Karen Foner from QVC for asking me to "do it all over again." Being chosen as a Today's Special Value last year is one of the greatest honors my recipes will ever receive. Then, to get to come back this year with another set of books—my feelings go beyond words.

Angela Miller and Coleen O'Shea, for helping me "think my future" and in doing so, helping me carve out the time to do what I love to do . . . create my recipes and write my words.

Shirley Morrow, Laura Powell, and Janelle Davis, for typing, typing, and typing some more. You'd think that by now I'd have learned to spell!

Rita Ahlers, Dee Ewing, and Janis Jackson, for helping me test and retest the recipes. Yes, it's fun, but it's also work, especially when it comes time to do the dishes.

Lori Hansen, for calculating the nutrient values of the recipes. It's a good thing she loves the computer as much as I love creating.

Rose Hoenig, R.D., L.D., for reviewing the recipes and calculating the Diabetic Exchanges. Even though she's busy, she finds the quality time needed to give my recipes the "okay" before I share them with others.

Barbara Alpert, for helping me organize my material so it's easier for everyone not only to use the recipes but also to read the books. I don't think I could find a better writing partner in all of "recipe land."

Cliff Lund, my Truck Drivin' Man and taste tester. He lets me know in no uncertain terms what he likes and what he doesn't like. And he likes **these recipes!**

Everyone who stopped in at JO's Kitchen Cafe for lunch while we were testing and was asked to sample a new dish. Some remarked that we were giving them the "tips," instead of the other way around.

God, for giving me the talent to create my "common folk" healthy recipes and to write in my "Grandma Moses" style. When I was given a lemon, He showed me how to make lemonade.

Grandma's Comfort Food—

Made Healthy

Why Grandma's Food Tasted So Good

Close your eyes and think back to when you were a little child and shared a meal at Grandma's table. Don't all those cozy feelings just rush right back into your heart? Grandma not only fed our mouths and tummies, she fed our spirits as well. With every bite we took, we were warmed by the love Grandma was sharing with us. She knew exactly what we liked best, and she always had it waiting for us when we visited. Maybe our parents wouldn't let us drink coffee, but Grandma would stir us up a glass of coffee-flavored milk and smile as we drank it with gusto. Cookies may have been off limits at home until homework was done, but at her house, the cookie jar was always brimming with our favorites—and studying was something we promised to do later!

Grandma knew that our food had to smell delicious, look scrumptious, and taste really good. Her cookies had to crunch "good" too, because we eat with all our senses. We eat with our noses, our eyes, our mouths, and our ears. That's why the little things you do when you prepare food make such a big difference to your loved ones. How much longer does it take to sprinkle a tablespoon of mini chocolate chips over the top of one of my pies? Maybe 15 seconds. But everyone you serve it to will think you went the extra mile just to please them. Sounds like something Grandma would do, doesn't it?

When preparing my "common folk" healthy recipes, you may be tempted to leave off those few chocolate chips (or other garnishes, like nuts) to save a few calories, a few pennies, or a few seconds. But please don't! When you share my recipes with your friends and family, they'll know that you stirred the lovin' into the cookin', and they'll remember your time together with cozy feelings—just like you remember those great meals at Grandma's house.

But what if you don't have any cozy family traditions of your own? What if your grandma devoted herself more to her garden than her kitchen? What if your mother worked full-time or went to school while you were young? What if your memories of family meals involve breakfasts grabbed on the run, fast-food lunches, drive-through dinners—and few of the warm recollections I feel lucky to have myself?

Start now.

Create your own wonderful rituals of togetherness around the table. Find ways to share food and feelings that mean something to you and your family. If you live alone, invite close friends to join you for holiday celebrations or just any time at all. Start a weekly supper club with neighbors and take turns making dinner or dessert. Pass along favorite recipes, perhaps written out beautifully on a card or pretty stationery, and choose some of my recipes to make your own.

What do I mean by that? Select a few main dishes and several desserts that you especially enjoy eating and sharing. Start bringing them to parties you attend and when you visit friends. Fill a basket with the ingredients of your favorite recipe and present it to a new neighbor as a housewarming gift. (Isn't that a lovely word—*housewarming*? It's a perfect way to describe creating an environment where people share food and affection!)

It's also not too late to share these new traditions with your own family, even if you are spread all over the country. Why not organize a family reunion, even if no one's ever done it, or invite everyone you know to an annual potluck at the lake? For many families, especially those where some marriages have ended in divorce and relationships can be complex, it's more important than ever to establish family ties and sustain them in every way we can.

I often talk about the "Healthy Exchanges Family," because I do feel that all of those who use my recipes—my QVC friends, my newsletter subscribers, the visitors to JO's Kitchen Cafe, and everyone who's purchased my books—are a kind of family, seated around a great table, and sharing the pleasures of good food along with the joys of good health. So believe me when I tell you that you are welcome as a member of my very big extended family, and I hope that the recipes in this volume will become your own favorite comfort foods—even if *I'm* the "grandma" who shared them with you!

Dear Friends,

People often ask me why I include the same general information at the beginning of all my cookbooks. If you've seen any of my other books, you'll know that my "common folk" recipes are just one part of the Healthy Exchanges picture. You know that I firmly believe—and say so whenever and wherever I can—that *Healthy Exchanges is not a diet, it's a way of life!* That's why I include the story of Healthy Exchanges in every book, because I know that the tale of my struggle to lose weight and regain my health is one that speaks to the hearts of many thousands of people. And because Healthy Exchanges is not just a collection of recipes, I always include the wisdom that I've learned from my own experiences and the knowledge of the health and cooking professionals I meet. Whether it's learning about nutrition or making shopping and cooking easier, no Healthy Exchanges book would be complete without features like "A Peek into My Pantry" or "JoAnna's Ten Commandments of Successful Cooking."

Even if you've read my other books you still might want to skim the following chapters—you never know when I'll slip in a new bit of wisdom or suggest a new product that will make your journey to health an easier and tastier one. If you're sharing this book with a friend or family member, you'll want to make sure they read the following pages before they start stirring up the recipes.

If this is the first book of mine that you've read, I want to welcome you with all my heart to the Healthy Exchanges Family. (And, of course, I'd love to hear your comments or questions. See the back of this book for my mailing address . . . or come visit if you happen to find yourself in DeWitt, Iowa—just ask anybody for directions to Healthy Exchanges!)

JoAnna

JoAnna M. Lund

and Healthy

Exchanges

Food is the first invited guest to every special occasion in every family's memory scrapbook. From baptism to graduation, from weddings to wakes, food brings us together.

It wasn't always that way at our house. I used to eat alone, even when my family was there, because while they were dining on real food, I was always nibbling at whatever my newest diet called for. In fact, for twenty-eight years I called myself the diet queen of DeWitt, Iowa.

I tried every diet I ever heard of, every one I could afford, and every one that found its way to my small town in eastern Iowa. I was willing to try anything that promised to "melt off the pounds," determined to deprive my body in every possible way in order to become thin at last.

I sent away for expensive "miracle" diet pills. I starved myself on the Cambridge Diet and the Bahama Diet. I gobbled Ayds diet candies, took thyroid pills, fiber pills, prescription and over-the-counter diet pills. I went to endless weight-loss support group meetings—but I somehow managed to turn healthy programs such as Overeaters Anonymous, Weight Watchers, and TOPS into unhealthy diets . . . diets I could never follow for more than a few months.

I was determined to discover something that worked long-term, but each new failure increased my desperation that I'd never find it.

I ate strange concoctions and rubbed on even stranger potions. I tried liquid diets like Slimfast and Metrecal. I agreed to be hypnotized. I tried reflexology and even had an acupuncture device stuck in my ear!

Does my story sound a lot like yours? I'm not surprised. No wonder the weight-loss business is a billion-dollar industry!

Every new thing I tried seemed to work—at least at first. And losing that first five or ten pounds would get me so excited, I'd believe that this new miracle diet would, finally, get my weight off for keeps.

Inevitably, though, the initial excitement wore off. The diet's routine and boredom set in, and I quit. I shoved the pills to the back of the medicine chest; pushed the cans of powdered shake mix to the rear of the kitchen cabinets; slid all the program materials out of sight under my bed; and once more I felt like a failure.

Like most dieters, I quickly gained back the weight I'd lost each time, along with a few extra "souvenir" pounds that seemed always to settle around my hips. I'd done the diet-lose-weight-gain-it-all-back "yo-yo" on the average of once a year. It's no exaggeration to say that over the years I've lost 1,000 pounds—and gained back 1,150 pounds.

Finally, at the age of 46 I weighed more than I'd ever imagined possible. I'd stopped believing that any diet could work for me. I drowned my sorrows in sacks of cake donuts and wondered if I'd live long enough to watch my grandchildren grow up.

Something had to change.

I had to change.

Finally, I did.

I'm just over 50 now—and I'm 130 pounds less than my all-time high of close to 300 pounds. I've kept the weight off for more than six years. I'd like to lose another ten pounds, but I'm not obsessed about it. If it takes me two or three years to accomplish it, that's okay.

What I *do* care about is never saying hello again to any of those unwanted pounds I said good-bye to!

How did I jump off the roller coaster I was on? For one thing, I finally stopped looking to food to solve my emotional problems. But what really shook me up—and got me started on the path that changed my life—was Operation Desert Storm in early 1991. I sent three children off to the Persian Gulf War—my son-in-law, Matt, a medic in Special Forces; my daughter, Becky, a full-time college student and member of a medical unit in the Army Reserve; and my son, James, a member of the Inactive Army Reserve reactivated as a chemicals expert.

Somehow, knowing that my children were putting their lives on the line got me thinking about my own mortality—and I knew in my heart the last thing they needed while they were overseas was to get a letter from home saying that their mother was ill because of a food-related problem.

The day I drove the third child to the airport to leave for Saudi Arabia, something happened to me that would change my life for the better—and forever. I stopped praying my constant prayer as a professional dieter, which was simply "Please, God, let me lose ten pounds by Friday." Instead, I began praying, "God, please help me not to be a burden to my kids and my family." I quit praying for what I wanted and started praying for what I needed—and in the process my prayers were answered. I couldn't keep the kids safe—that was out of my hands—but I could try to get healthier to better handle the stress of it. It was the least I could do on the home front.

That quiet prayer was the beginning of the new JoAnna Lund. My initial goal was not to lose weight or create healthy recipes. I only wanted to become healthier for my kids, my husband, and myself.

Each of my children returned safely from the Persian Gulf War. But something didn't come back—the 130 extra pounds I'd been lugging around for far too long. I'd finally accepted the truth after all those agonizing years of suffering through on-again, off-again dieting.

There are no "magic" cures in life.

No "magic" potion, pill, or diet will make unwanted pounds disappear.

I found something better than magic, if you can believe it. When I turned my weight and health dilemma over to God for guidance, a new JoAnna Lund and Healthy Exchanges were born.

I discovered a new way to live my life—and uncovered an unexpected talent for creating easy "common folk" healthy recipes, and sharing my commonsense approach to healthy living. I learned that I could motivate others to change their lives and adopt a positive outlook. I began publishing cookbooks and a monthly food newsletter, and speaking to groups all over the country.

I like to say, *"When life handed me a lemon, not only did I make healthy, tasty lemonade, I wrote the recipe down!"*

What I finally found was not a quick fix or a short-term diet, but a great way to live well for a lifetime.

I want to share it with you.

Healthy Exchanges®
Weight Loss
Choices™/Exchanges

If you've ever been on one of the national weight-loss programs like Weight Watchers or Diet Center, you've already been introduced to the concept of measured portions of different food groups that make up your daily food plan. If you are not familiar with such a system of weight-loss choices or exchanges, here's a brief explanation. (If you want or need more detailed information, you can write to the American Dietetic Association or the American Diabetes Association for comprehensive explanations.)

The idea of food exchanges is to divide foods into basic food groups. The foods in each group are measured in servings that have comparable values. These groups include Proteins/Meats, Breads/Starches, Vegetables, Fats, Fruits, Skim Milk, Free Foods, and Optional Calories.

Each choice or exchange included in a particular group has about the same number of calories and a similar carbohydrate, protein, and fat content as the other foods in that group. Because any food on a particular list can be "exchanged" for any other food in that group, it makes sense to call the food groups *exchanges* or *choices*.

I like to think we are also "exchanging" bad habits and food choices for good ones!

By using Weight Loss Choices™ or exchanges you can choose from a variety of foods without having to calculate the nutrient value of each one. This makes it easier to include a wide variety of foods in your daily menus and gives you the opportunity to tailor your choices to your unique appetite.

If you want to lose weight, you should consult your physician or other weight-control expert regarding the number of servings that would be best for you from each food group. Since men generally require more calories than women, and since the requirements for growing children and teenagers differ from those for adults, the right number of exchanges for any one person is a personal decision.

I have included a suggested plan of weight-loss choices in the pages following the exchange lists. It's a program I used to lose 130 pounds, and it's the one I still follow today.

(If you are a diabetic or have been diagnosed with heart problems, it is best to meet with your physician before using this or any other food program or recipe collection.)

Food Group Weight Loss Choices™/Exchanges

Not all food group exchanges are alike. The ones that follow are for anyone who's interested in weight loss or maintenance. Diabetic exchanges are calculated by the American Diabetic Association, and information about them is provided in *The Diabetic's Healthy Exchanges Cookbook* (Perigee Books).

Every Healthy Exchanges recipe provides calculations in three ways:

- Weight Loss Choices/Exchanges

- Calories, Fat, Protein, Carbohydrates, and Fiber Grams, and Sodium in milligrams

- Diabetic Exchanges calculated for me by a Registered Dietitian

Healthy Exchanges recipes can help you eat well and recover your health, whatever your health concerns may be. Please take a few minutes to review the exchange lists and the suggestions that follow on how to count them. You have lots of great eating in store for you!

Proteins

Meat, poultry, seafood, eggs, cheese, and legumes.

One exchange of Protein is approximately 60 calories. Examples of one Protein choice or exchange:

1 ounce cooked weight of lean meat, poultry, or seafood

2 ounces white fish

1½ ounces 97% fat-free ham

1 egg (limit to no more than 4 per week)

¼ cup egg substitute

3 egg whites

¾ ounce reduced-fat cheese

½ cup fat-free cottage cheese

2 ounces cooked or ¾ ounce uncooked dry beans

1 tablespoon peanut butter (also count 1 fat exchange)

Breads

Breads, crackers, cereals, grains, and starchy vegetables. One exchange of Bread is approximately 80 calories. Examples of 1 Bread choice or exchange:

1 slice bread or 2 slices reduced-calorie bread (40 calories or less)

1 roll, any type (1 ounce)

½ cup cooked pasta or ¾ ounce uncooked (scant ½ cup)

½ cup cooked rice or 1 ounce uncooked (⅓ cup)

3 tablespoons flour

¾ ounce cold cereal

½ cup cooked hot cereal or ¾ ounce uncooked (2 tablespoons)

½ cup corn (kernels or cream-style) or peas

4 ounces white potato, cooked, or 5 ounces uncooked

3 ounces sweet potato, cooked, or 4 ounces uncooked

3 cups air-popped popcorn

7 fat-free crackers (¾ ounce)

3 (2½-inch squares) graham crackers

2 (¾-ounce) rice cakes or 6 mini

1 tortilla, any type (6-inch diameter)

Fruits

All fruits and fruit juices. One exchange of Fruit is approximately 60 calories. Examples of one Fruit choice or exchange:

1 small apple or ½ cup slices
1 small orange
½ medium banana
¾ cup berries (except strawberries and cranberries)
1 cup strawberries or cranberries
½ cup canned fruit, packed in fruit juice or rinsed well
2 tablespoons raisins
1 tablespoon spreadable fruit spread
½ cup apple juice (4 fluid ounces)
½ cup orange juice (4 fluid ounces)
½ cup applesauce

Skim Milk

Milk, buttermilk, and yogurt. One exchange of Skim Milk is approximately 90 calories. Examples of one Skim Milk choice or exchange:

1 cup skim milk
½ cup evaporated skim milk
1 cup low-fat buttermilk
¾ cup plain fat-free yogurt
⅓ cup nonfat dry milk powder

Vegetables

All fresh, canned, or frozen vegetables other than the starchy vegetables. One exchange of Vegetable is approximately 30 calories. Examples of one Vegetable choice or exchange:

½ cup vegetable
¼ cup tomato sauce
1 medium fresh tomato
½ cup vegetable juice

Fats

Margarine, mayonnaise, vegetable oils, salad dressings, olives, and nuts. One exchange of fat is approximately 40 calories. Examples of one Fat choice or exchange:

1 teaspoon margarine or 2 teaspoons reduced-calorie margarine
1 teaspoon butter
1 teaspoon vegetable oil
1 teaspoon mayonnaise or 2 teaspoons reduced-calorie mayonnaise
1 teaspoon peanut butter
1 ounce olives
¼ ounce pecans or walnuts

Free Foods

Foods that do not provide nutritional value but are used to enhance the taste of foods are included in the Free Foods group. Examples of these are spices, herbs, extracts, vinegar, lemon juice, mustard, Worcestershire sauce, and soy sauce. Cooking sprays and artificial sweeteners used in moderation are also included in this group. However, you'll see that I include the caloric value of artificial sweeteners in the Optional Calories of the recipes.

You may occasionally see a recipe that lists "free food" as part of the portion. According to the published exchange lists, a free food contains fewer than 20 calories per serving. Two or three servings per day of free foods/drinks are usually allowed in a meal plan.

Optional Calories

Foods that do not fit into any other group but are used in moderation in recipes are included in Optional Calories. Foods that are counted in this way include sugar-free gelatin and puddings, fat-free mayonnaise and dressings, reduced-calorie whipped toppings, reduced-calorie syrups and jams, chocolate chips, coconut, and canned broth.

Sliders™

These are 80 Optional Calorie increments that do not fit into any particular category. You can choose which food group to *slide* these into. It is wise to limit this selection to approximately three to four per day to ensure the best possible nutrition for your body while still enjoying an occasional treat.

Sliders™ may be used in either of the following ways:

1. If you have consumed all your Protein, Bread, Fruit, or Skim Milk Weight Loss Choices for the day, and you want to eat addi-

tional foods from those food groups, you simply use a Slider. It's what I call "healthy horse trading." Remember that Sliders may not be traded for choices in the Vegetables or Fats food groups.

2. Sliders may also be deducted from your Optional Calories for the day or week. ¼ Slider equals 20 Optional Calories; ½ Slider equals 40 Optional Calories; ¾ Slider equals 60 Optional Calories; and 1 Slider equals 80 Optional Calories.

Healthy Exchanges® Weight Loss Choices™

My original Healthy Exchanges program of Weight Loss Choices™ was based on an average daily total of 1,400 to 1,600 calories per day. That was what I determined was right for my needs, and for those of most women. Because men require additional calories (about 1,600 to 1,900), here are my suggested plans for women and men. (*If you require more or fewer calories, please revise this plan to meet your individual needs.*)

Each day, women should plan to eat:

2 Skim Milk servings, 90 calories each
2 Fat servings, 40 calories each
3 Fruit servings, 60 calories each
4 Vegetable servings or more, 30 calories each
5 Protein servings, 60 calories each
5 Bread servings, 80 calories each

Each day, men should plan to eat:

2 Skim Milk servings, 90 calories each
4 Fat servings, 40 calories each
3 Fruit servings, 60 calories each
4 Vegetable servings or more, 30 calories each
6 Protein servings, 60 calories each
7 Bread servings, 80 calories each

Young people should follow the program for men but add 1 Skim Milk serving for a total of 3 servings.

You may also choose to add up to 100 Optional Calories per day, and up to 21 to 28 Sliders per week at 80 calories each. If you choose to include more Sliders in your daily or weekly totals, deduct those 80 calories from your Optional Calorie "bank."

A word about **Sliders™:** These are to be counted toward your totals after you have used your allotment of choices of Skim Milk, Protein, Bread, and Fruit for the day. By "sliding" an additional choice into one of these groups, you can meet your individual needs for that day. Sliders are especially helpful when traveling, stressed-out, eating out, or for special events. I often use mine so I can enjoy my favorite Healthy Exchanges desserts. Vegetables are not to be counted as Sliders. Enjoy as many Vegetable choices as you need to feel satisfied. Because we want to limit our fat intake to moderate amounts, additional Fat choices should not be counted as Sliders. If you choose to include more fat on an *occasional* basis, count the extra choices as Optional Calories.

Keep a daily food diary of your Weight Loss Choices, checking off what you eat as you go. If, at the end of the day, your required selections are not 100 percent accounted for, but you have done the best you can, go to bed with a clear conscience. There will be days when you have ¼ Fruit or ½ Bread left over. What are you going to do—eat two slices of an orange or half a slice of bread and throw the rest out? I always say that "nothing in life comes out exact." Just do the best you can . . . *the best you can.*

Try to drink at least eight 8-ounce glasses of water a day. Water truly is the "nectar" of good health.

As a little added insurance, I take a multivitamin each day. It's not essential, but if my day's worth of well-planned meals "bites the dust" when unexpected events intrude on my regular routine, my body still gets its vital nutrients.

The calories listed in each group of choices are averages. Some choices within each group may be higher or lower, so it's important to select a variety of different foods instead of eating the same three or four all the time.

Use your Optional Calories! They are what I call "life's little extras." They make all the difference in how you enjoy your food and appreciate the variety available to you. Yes, we can get by without them, but do you really want to? Keep in mind that you should be using all your daily Weight Loss Choices first to ensure you are getting the basics of good nutrition. But I guarantee that Optional Calories will keep you from feeling deprived—and help you reach your weight-loss goals.

Sodium, Fat, Cholesterol, and Processed Foods

Are Healthy Exchanges ingredients really healthy? When I first created Healthy Exchanges, many people asked about sodium, about whether it was necessary to calculate the percentage of fat, saturated fat, and cholesterol in a healthy diet, and about my use of processed foods in many recipes. I researched these questions as I was developing my program, so you can feel confident about using the recipes and food plan.

Sodium

Most people consume more sodium than their bodies need. The American Heart Association and the American Diabetes Association recommend limiting daily sodium intake to no more than 3,000 milligrams per day. If your doctor suggests you limit your sodium even more, then *you really must read labels.*

Sodium is an essential nutrient and should not be completely eliminated. It helps to regulate blood volume and is needed for normal daily muscle and nerve functions. Most of us, however, have no trouble getting "all we need" and then some.

As with everything else, moderation is my approach. I rarely ever have salt in my list as an added ingredient. But if you're especially sodium-sensitive, make the right choices for you—and save high-sodium foods such as sauerkraut for an occasional treat.

I use lots of spices to enhance flavors, so you won't notice the absence of salt. In the few cases where it is used, salt is vital for the success of the recipe, so please don't omit it.

When I do use an ingredient high in sodium, I try to compensate by using low-sodium products in the remainder of the recipe. Many fat-free products are a little higher in sodium to make up for any loss of flavor that disappeared along with the fat. But when I take advantage of these fat-free, higher-sodium products, I stretch that ingredient within the recipe, lowering the amount of sodium per serving. A good example is my use of fat-free and reduced-sodium canned soups. While the suggested number of servings per can is 2, I make sure my final creation serves at least 4 and sometimes 6. So the soup's sodium has been "watered down" from one-third to one-half of the original amount.

Even if you don't have to watch your sodium intake for medical reasons, using moderation is another "healthy exchange" to make on your own journey to good health.

Fat Percentages

We've been told that 30 percent is the magic number—that we should limit fat intake to 30 percent or less of our total calories. It's good advice, and I try to have a weekly average of 15 percent to 25 percent myself. I believe any less than 15 percent is really just another restrictive diet that won't last. And more than 25 percent on a regular basis is too much of a good thing.

When I started listing fat grams along with calories in my recipes, I was tempted to include the percentage of calories from fat. After all, in the vast majority of my recipes, that percentage is well below 30 percent This even includes my pie recipes that allow you a realistic serving instead of many "diet" recipes that tell you a serving is one-twelfth of a pie.

Figuring fat grams is easy enough. Each gram of fat equals 9 calories. Multiply fat grams by 9, then divide that number by the total calories to get the percentage of calories from fat.

So why don't I do it? After consulting four registered dietitians for advice, I decided to omit this information. They felt that it's too easy for people to become obsessed by that 30 percent figure, which is after all supposed to be a percentage of total calories over the course of a day or a week. We mustn't feel we can't include a healthy ingredient such as pecans or olives in one recipe just because, on its own, it has more than 30 percent of its calories from fat.

An example of this would be a casserole made with 90 percent lean red meat. Most of us benefit from eating red meat in moderation, as it provides iron and niacin in our diets, and it also makes life more enjoyable for us and those who eat with us. If we *only* look at the percentage of calories from fat in a serving of this one dish, which might be as high as 40 to 45 percent, we might choose not to include this recipe in our weekly food plan.

The dietitians suggested that it's important to consider the total picture when making such decisions. As long as your overall food plan keeps fat calories to 30 percent, it's all right to enjoy an occasional dish that is somewhat higher in fat content. Healthy foods I include in **MODERATION** include 90 percent lean red meat, olives, and nuts. I don't eat these foods every day, and you may not either. But occasionally, in a good recipe, they make all the difference in the world between just getting by (deprivation) and truly enjoying your food.

Remember, the goal is eating in a healthy way so you can enjoy and live well the rest of your life.

Saturated Fats and Cholesterol

You'll see that I don't provide calculations for saturated fats or cholesterol amounts in my recipes. It's for the simple and yet not so simple reason that accurate, up-to-date, brand-specific information can be difficult to obtain from food manufacturers, especially since the way in which they produce food keeps changing rapidly. But once more I've consulted with Registered Dietitians and other professionals and found that, because I use only a few products that are high in saturated fat, and use them in such limited quantities, my recipes are suitable for patients concerned about controlling or lowering cholesterol. You'll also find that whenever I do use one of these ingredients *in moderation*, everything else in the recipe, and in the meals my family and I enjoy, is low in fat.

Processed Foods

Just what *is* processed food, anyway? What do I mean by the term "processed food," and why do I use them when the "purest" recipe developers in Recipe Land consider them "pedestrian" and won't ever use something from a box, container, or can? A letter I received and a passing statement from a stranger made me reflect on what I mean when I refer to processed foods, and helped me reaffirm why I use them in my "common folk" healthy recipes.

If you are like the vast millions who agree with me, then I'm not sharing anything new with you. And if you happen to disagree, that's okay, too. After all, this is America, the Land of the Free. We are blessed to live in a great nation where we can all believe what we want about anything.

A few months go, a woman sent me several articles from various "whole food" publications and wrote that she was wary of processed foods, and wondered why I used them in my recipes. She then scribbled on the bottom of her note, "Just how healthy *is* Healthy Exchanges?" Then, a few weeks later, during a chance visit at a public food event with a very pleasant woman, I was struck by how we all have our own definitions of what processed foods are. She shared with me, in a somewhat self-righteous manner, that she *never* uses processed foods. She only cooked with fresh fruits and vegetables, she told me. Then later she said that she used canned reduced-fat soups all the time! Was her definition different than mine, I wondered? Soup in a can, whether it's reduced in fat or not, still meets my definition of a processed food.

So I got out a copy of my book *HELP: Healthy Exchanges Lifetime Plan*, and reread what I had written back then about processed foods. Nothing in my definition had changed since I wrote that section. I still believe that healthy processed foods, such as canned soups, prepared piecrusts, sugar-free instant puddings, nonfat sour cream, and frozen whipped topping, when used properly, all have a place as ingredients in healthy recipes.

I never use an ingredient that hasn't been approved by either the American Diabetic Association, the American Dietetic Association, or the American Heart Association. Whenever I'm in doubt, I send for their position papers, then ask knowledgeable registered dietitians to explain those papers to me in "street language." I've been assured by all of them that the sugar- and fat-free products I use in my recipes are indeed safe.

If you don't agree, nothing I can say or write will convince you otherwise. But, if you've been using the healthy processed foods and have been concerned about the almost daily hoopla you hear about yet another product that's about the doom of all of us, then just stay with reason. For every product on the grocery shelves, there are those who want you to buy it and there are those who don't, *because they want you to buy their products instead.* So we have to learn to sift the fact from the fiction. Let's take sugar substitutes, for example. In making our own evaluations, we should toss out any information provided by the sugar substitute manufacturers, because they have a vested interest in our buying their products. Likewise, we should toss out any information provided by the sugar industry, because they have a vested interest in our not buying sugar substitutes. Then, if you aren't sure if you can really trust the government or any of its agencies, toss out their data, too. That leaves the three associations I mentioned above. Do you think any of them would say a product is safe if it isn't? Or say a product isn't safe when it is? They have nothing to gain or lose, *other than their integrity,* if they intentionally try to mislead us. That's why I only go to these associations for information concerning healthy processed foods.

I certainly don't recommend that everything we eat comes from a can, box, or jar. I think the best of all possible worlds is to start with the basics: grains such as rice, pasta, or corn. Then, for example, add some raw vegetables and extra-lean meat such as poultry, fish, beef, or pork. Stir in some healthy canned soup or tomato sauce, and you'll end up with something that is not only healthy but tastes so good, everyone from toddlers to great-grand-parents will want to eat it!

I've never been in favor of spraying everything we eat with chemicals and I don't believe that all our foods should come out of packages. But I do think we should use the best available healthy processed foods to make cooking easier and food taste better. I take advantage of the good-tasting low-fat and low-sugar products found in any grocery store. My recipes are created for busy people like me, people who want to eat healthily and economically but who still want the food to satisfy their taste buds. I don't expect any-one to visit out-of-the-way health food stores or find the time to cook beans from scratch—*because I don't!* Most of you can't grow fresh food in the backyard and many of you may not have access to farmers' markets or large supermarkets. I want to help you figure out realistic ways to make healthy eating a reality *wherever you live*, or you will not stick to a healthy lifestyle for long.

So if you've been swayed (by individuals or companies with vested interests or hidden agendas) into thinking that all processed foods are bad for you, you may want to reconsider your position. Or if you've been fooling yourself into believing that you *never* use processed foods but regularly reach for that healthy canned soup, stop playing games with yourself—you are using processed foods in a healthy way. And, if you're like me and use healthy processed foods in *moderation*, don't let anyone make you feel ashamed about including these products in your healthy lifestyle. Only *you* can decide what's best for *you* and your family's needs.

Part of living a healthy lifestyle is making those decisions and then getting on with life. Congratulations on choosing to live a healthy lifestyle, and let's celebrate together by sharing a piece of Healthy Exchanges pie that I've garnished with Cool Whip Lite!

JoAnna's Ten Commandments of Successful Cooking

A very important part of any journey is knowing where you are going and the best way to get there. If you plan and prepare before you start to cook, you should reach mealtime with foods to write home about!

1. **Read the entire recipe from start to finish** and be sure you understand the process involved. Check that you have all the equipment you will need *before* you begin.

2. **Check the ingredient list** and be sure you have *everything* and in the amounts required. Keep cooking sprays handy—while they're not listed as ingredients, I use them all the time (just a quick squirt!).

3. **Set out *all*** the ingredients and equipment needed to prepare the recipe on the counter near you *before* you start. Remember that old saying, *A stitch in time saves nine?* It applies in the kitchen, too.

4. **Do as much advance preparation as possible** before actually cooking. Chop, cut, grate, or whatever is needed

to prepare the ingredients and have them ready before you start to mix. Turn the oven on at least ten minutes before putting food in to bake, to allow the oven to preheat to the proper temperature.

5. **Use a kitchen timer** to tell you when the cooking or baking time is up. Because stove temperatures vary slightly by manufacturer, you may want to set your timer for five minutes less than the suggested time just to prevent overcooking. Check the progress of your dish at that time, then decide if you need the additional minutes or not.

6. **Measure carefully.** Use glass measures for liquids and metal or plastic cups for dry ingredients. My recipes are based on standard measurements. Unless I tell you it's a scant or full cup, measure the cup level.

7. **For best results, follow the recipe instructions exactly.** Feel free to substitute ingredients that *don't tamper* with the basic chemistry of the recipe, but be sure to leave key ingredients alone. For example, you could substitute sugar-free instant chocolate pudding for sugar-free butterscotch instant pudding, but if you used a six-serving package when a four-serving package was listed in the ingredients, or you used instant when cook-and-serve is required, you won't get the right result.

8. **Clean up as you go.** It is much easier to wash a few items at a time than to face a whole counter of dirty dishes later. The same is true for spills on the counter or floor.

9. **Be careful about doubling or halving a recipe.** Though many recipes can be altered successfully to serve more or fewer people, *many cannot*. This is especially true when it comes to spices and liquids. If you try to double a recipe that calls for 1 teaspoon pumpkin-pie spice, for example, and you double the spice, you may end up with a too-spicy taste. I usually suggest increasing spices or liquid by 1 ½ times when doubling a recipe. If it tastes a little bland to you, you can increase the spice to 1 ¾ times the original amount the next time you prepare the dish. Remember: You can always add more, but you can't take it out after it's stirred in.

The same is true with liquid ingredients. If you wanted to **triple** a recipe like my **Zucchini Marinara Spaghetti** because you were planning to serve a crowd, you might think you should use three times as much of every ingredient. Don't, or you could end up with Zucchini Marinara Spaghetti Soup! The original recipe calls for 1¾ cups of chunky tomato sauce, so I'd suggest using 3½ cups when you **triple** the recipe (or 2¾ cups if you **double** it). You'll still have a good-tasting dish that won't run all over the plate.

10. **Write your reactions next to each recipe once you've served it.** Yes, that's right, I'm giving you permission to write in this book. It's yours, after all. Ask yourself: Did everyone like it? Did you have to add another half teaspoon of chili seasoning to please your family, who like to live on the spicier side of the street? You may even want to rate the recipe on a scale of 1★ to 4★, depending on what you thought of it. (Four stars would be the top rating—and I hope you'll feel that way about many of my recipes.) Jotting down your comments while they are fresh in your mind will help you personalize the recipe to your own taste the next time you prepare it.

My Best Healthy Exchanges Tips and Tidbits

Measurements, General Cooking Tips, and Basic Ingredients

The word *moderation* best describes **my use of fats, sugar substitutes,** and **sodium** in these recipes. Wherever possible, I've used cooking spray for sautéing and for browning meats and vegetables. I also use reduced-calorie margarine and no-fat mayonnaise and salad dressings. Lean ground turkey *or* ground beef can be used in the recipes. Just be sure whatever you choose is at least *90 percent lean.*

I've also included **small amounts of sugar and brown sugar substitutes as the sweetening agent** in many of the recipes. I don't drink a hundred cans of soda a day or eat enough artificially sweetened foods in a 24-hour time period to be troubled by sugar substitutes. But if this is a concern of yours and you *do not* need to watch your sugar intake, you can always replace the sugar substitutes with processed sugar and the sugar-free products with regular ones.

I created my recipes knowing they would also be used by hypoglycemics, diabetics, and those concerned about triglycerides. If you choose to use sugar instead, be sure to count the additional calories.

A word of caution when cooking with **sugar substitutes**: Use saccharin-based sweeteners when **heating or baking**. In recipes that **don't require heat, Aspartame** (known as Nutrasweet) works well in uncooked dishes but leaves an aftertaste in baked products.

I'm often asked why I use an **8-by-8-inch baking dish** in my recipes. It's for portion control. If the recipe says it serves 4, just cut down the center, turn the dish, and cut again. Like magic, there's your serving. Also, if this is the only recipe you are preparing requiring an oven, the square dish fits into a tabletop toaster oven easily and energy can be conserved.

To make life even easier, **whenever a recipe calls for ounce measurements** (other than raw meats) I've included the closest cup equivalent. I need to use my scale daily when creating recipes, so I've measured for you at the same time.

Most of the recipes are for **4 to 6 servings**. If you don't have that many to feed, do what I do: freeze individual portions. Then all you have to do is choose something from the freezer and take it to work for lunch or have your evening meals prepared in advance for the week. In this way, I always have something on hand that is both good to eat and good for me.

Unless a recipe includes hard-boiled eggs, cream cheese, mayonnaise, or a raw vegetable or fruit, **the leftovers should freeze well**. (I've marked recipes that freeze well with the symbol of a **snowflake✳**.)This includes most of the cream pies. Divide any recipe up into individual servings and freeze for your own "TV" dinners.

Another good idea is **cutting leftover pie into individual pieces and freezing each one separately** in a small Ziploc freezer bag. Then the next time you want to thaw a piece of pie for yourself, you don't have to thaw the whole pie. It's great this way for brown-bag lunches, too. Just pull a piece out of the freezer on your way to work and by lunchtime you will have a wonderful dessert waiting for you.

Unless I specify **"covered" for simmering or baking**, prepare my recipes **uncovered**. Occasionally you will read a recipe that asks you to cover a dish for a time, then to uncover, so read the directions carefully to avoid confusion—and to get the best results.

Low-fat cooking spray is another blessing in a Healthy Exchanges kitchen. It's currently available in three flavors . . .

•**OLIVE-OIL FLAVORED** when cooking Mexican, Italian, or Greek dishes

•**BUTTER FLAVORED** when the hint of butter is desired

•**REGULAR** for everything else.

A quick spray of butter flavored makes air-popped popcorn a low-fat taste treat, or try it as a butter substitute on steaming hot corn on the cob. One light spray of the skillet when browning meat will convince you that you're using "old-fashioned fat," and a quick coating of the casserole dish before you add the ingredients will make serving easier and cleanup quicker.

I use reduced-sodium **canned chicken broth** in place of dry bouillon to lower the sodium content. The intended flavor is still present in the prepared dish. As a reduced-sodium beef broth is not currently available (at least not in DeWitt, Iowa), I use the canned regular beef broth. The sodium content is still lower than regular dry bouillon.

Whenever **cooked rice or pasta** is an ingredient, follow the package directions, but eliminate the salt and/or margarine called for. This helps lower the sodium and fat content. It tastes just fine; trust me on this.

Here's another tip: When **cooking rice or noodles**, why not cook extra "for the pot"? After you use what you need, store leftover rice in a covered container (where it will keep for a couple of days). With noodles like spaghetti or macaroni, first rinse and drain as usual, then measure out what you need. Put the leftovers in a bowl covered with water, then store in the refrigerator, covered, until they're needed. Then, measure out what you need, rinse and drain them, and they're ready to go.

Does your **pita bread** often tear before you can make a sandwich? Here's my tip to make them open easily: cut the bread in half, put the halves in the microwave for about 15 seconds, and they will open up by themselves. *Voilà!*

When **chunky salsa** is listed as an ingredient, I leave the degree of "heat" up to your personal taste. In our house, I'm considered a wimp. I go for the "mild" while Cliff prefers "extra-hot." How do we compromise? I prepare the recipe with mild salsa because he can always add a spoonful or two of the hotter version to his serving, but I can't enjoy the dish if it's too spicy for me.

Milk and Yogurt

Take it from me—nonfat dry milk powder is great! I *do not* use it for drinking, but I *do* use it for cooking. Three good reasons why:

(1) It is very **inexpensive**.

(2) It **does not sour** because you use it only as needed. Store the box in your refrigerator or freezer and it will keep almost forever.

(3) You can easily **add extra calcium** to just about any recipe without added liquid. I consider nonfat dry milk powder one of Mother Nature's modern-day miracles of convenience. But do purchase a good national name brand (I like Carnation), and keep it fresh by proper storage.

In many of my pies and puddings, I use nonfat dry milk powder and water instead of skim milk. Usually I call for ⅔ cup nonfat dry milk powder and 1¼ to 1½ cups water or liquid. This way I can get the nutrients of two cups of milk, but much less liquid, and the end result is much creamier. Also, the recipe sets up quicker, usually in 5 minutes or less. So if someone knocks at your door unexpectedly at mealtime, you can quickly throw a pie together and enjoy it minutes later.

You can make your own "**sour cream**" by combining ¾ cup plain fat-free yogurt with ⅓ cup nonfat dry milk powder. What you did by doing this is fourfold: 1) The dry milk stabilizes the yogurt and keeps the whey from separating. 2) The dry milk slightly helps to cut the tartness of the yogurt. 3) It's still virtually fat-free. 4) The calcium has been increased by 100 percent. Isn't it great how we can make that distant relative of sour cream a first kissin' cousin by adding the nonfat dry milk powder? Or, if you place 1 cup of plain fat-free yogurt in a sieve lined with a coffee filter, and place the sieve over a small bowl and refrigerate for about 6 hours, you will end up with a very good alternative for sour cream. To **stabilize yogurt** when cooking or baking with it, just add 1 teaspoon cornstarch to every ¾ cup yogurt.

If a recipe calls for **evaporated skim milk** and you don't have any in the cupboard, make your own. For every ½ cup evaporated skim milk needed, combine ⅓ cup nonfat dry milk powder and ½ cup water. Use as you would evaporated skim milk.

You can also make your own **sugar-free and fat-free sweetened condensed milk** at home. Combine 1⅓ cups nonfat dry milk powder and ½ cup cold water in a 2-cup glass measure. Cover and microwave on HIGH until mixture is hot but *not* boiling. Stir in ½ cup Sprinkle Sweet or Sugar Twin. Cover and refrigerate at least 4 hours. This mixture will keep for up to 2 weeks in the refrigerator. Use in just about any recipe that calls for sweetened condensed milk.

For any recipe that calls for **buttermilk**, you might want to try JO's Buttermilk: Blend one cup of water and ⅔ cup dry milk powder (the nutrients of two cups of skim milk). It'll be thicker than this mixed-up milk usually is, because it's doubled. Add 1 teaspoon white vinegar and stir, then let it sit for at least 10 minutes.

One of my subscribers was looking for a way to further restrict salt intake, and needed a substitute for **cream of mushroom soup**. For many of my recipes, I use Healthy Request Cream of Mushroom Soup, as it is a reduced-sodium product. The label suggests 2 servings per can, but I usually incorporate the soup into a recipe serving at least four. By doing this, I've reduced the sodium in the soup by half again.

But if you must restrict your sodium even more, try making my Healthy Exchanges **Creamy Mushroom Sauce**. Place 1½ cups evaporated skim milk and 3 tablespoons flour in a covered jar. Shake well and pour mixture into a medium saucepan sprayed with butter-flavored cooking spray. Add ½ cup canned sliced mushrooms, rinsed and drained. Cook over medium heat, stirring often, until mixture thickens. Add any seasonings of your choice. You can use this sauce in any recipe that calls for one 10 ¾-ounce can of cream of mushroom soup.

Why did I choose these proportions and ingredients?

- 1½ cups evaporated skim milk is the amount in one can.

- It's equal to three milk choices or exchanges.

- It's the perfect amount of liquid and flour for a medium cream sauce.

- 3 tablespoons flour is equal to one bread/starch choice or exchange.

- Any leftovers will reheat beautifully with a flour-based sauce, but not with a cornstarch base.

- The mushrooms are one vegetable choice or exchange.

- This sauce is virtually fat-free, sugar-free, and sodium-free.

Proteins

I use eggs in moderation. I enjoy the real thing on an average of three to four times a week. So, my recipes are calculated on using whole eggs. However, if you choose to use egg substitute in place of the egg, the finished product will turn out just fine and the fat grams per serving will be even lower than those listed.

If you like the look, taste, and feel of **hard-boiled eggs** in salads but haven't been using them because of the cholesterol in the yolk, I have a couple of alternatives for you. 1) Pour an 8-ounce carton of egg substitute into a medium skillet sprayed with cooking spray. Cover skillet tightly and cook over low heat until substitute is just set, about 10 minutes. Remove from heat and let set, still covered, for 10 minutes more. Uncover and cool completely. Chop set mixture. This will make about 1 cup of chopped egg. 2) Even easier is to hard-boil "real eggs," toss the yolk away, and chop the white. Either way, you don't deprive yourself of the pleasure of egg in your salad.

In most recipes calling for **egg substitutes**, you can use 2 egg whites in place of the equivalent of 1 egg substitute. Just break the eggs open and toss the yolks away. I can hear some of you already saying, "But that's wasteful!" Well, take a look at the price on the egg substitute package (which usually has the equivalent of 4 eggs in it), then look at the price of a dozen eggs, from which you'd get the equivalent of 6 egg substitutes. Now, what's wasteful about that?

Whenever I include **cooked chicken** in a recipe, I use roasted white meat without skin. Whenever I include **roast beef or pork** in a recipe, I use the loin cuts because they are much leaner. However, most of the time, I do my roasting of all these meats at the local deli. I just ask for a chunk of their lean roasted meat, 6 or 8 ounces, and ask them not to slice it. When I get home, I cube or dice the meat and am ready to use it in my recipe. The reason I do this is threefold: 1) I'm getting just the amount I need without leftovers; 2) I don't have the expense of heating the oven; and 3) I'm not throwing away the bone, gristle, and fat I'd be cutting away from the meat. Overall, it is probably cheaper to "roast" it the way I do.

Did you know that you can make an acceptable meat loaf without using egg for the binding? Just replace every egg with ¼ cup of liquid. You could use beef broth, tomato sauce, even applesauce, to name just a few. For a meat loaf to serve 6, I always use 1 pound of extra-lean ground beef or turkey, 6 tablespoons of dried fine bread crumbs, and ¼ cup of the liquid, plus anything else healthy that strikes my fancy at the time. I mix well and place the mixture in an 8-by-8-inch baking dish or 9-by-5-inch loaf pan sprayed with cooking spray. Bake uncovered at 350 degrees for 35 to 50 minutes (depending on the added ingredients). You will never miss the egg.

Any time you are **browning ground meat** for a casserole and want to get rid of almost all the excess fat, just place the uncooked meat loosely in a plastic colander. Set the colander in a glass pie plate. Place in microwave and cook on HIGH for 3 to 6 minutes (depending on the amount being browned), stirring often. Use as you would for any casserole. You can also chop up onions and brown them with the meat if you want.

Fruits and Vegetables

If you want to enjoy a **"fruit shake"** with some pizazz, just combine soda water and unsweetened fruit juice in a blender. Add crushed ice. Blend on HIGH until thick. Refreshment without guilt.

You'll see that many recipes use ordinary **canned vegetables**. They're much cheaper than reduced-sodium versions, and once you rinse and drain them, the sodium is reduced anyway. I believe in saving money wherever possible so we can afford the best fat-free and sugar-free products as they come onto the market.

All three kinds of **vegetables—fresh, frozen, and canned**—have their place in a healthy diet. My husband, Cliff, hates the taste of frozen or fresh green beans, thinks the texture is all wrong, so I use canned green beans instead. In this case, canned vegetables have their proper place when I'm feeding my husband. If someone in your family has a similar concern, it's important to respond to it so everyone can be happy and enjoy the meal.

When I use **fruits or vegetables** like apples, cucumbers, and zucchini, I wash them really well and **leave the skin on**. It provides added color, fiber, and attractiveness to any dish. And, because I use processed flour in my cooking, I like to increase the fiber in my diet by eating my fruits and vegetables in their closest-to-natural state.

To help keep **fresh fruits and veggies fresh**, just give them a quick "shower" with lemon juice. The easiest way to do this is to pour purchased lemon juice into a kitchen spray bottle and store in the refrigerator. Then, every time you use fresh fruits or vegetables in a salad or dessert, simply give them a quick spray with your "lemon spritzer." You just might be amazed by how this little trick keeps your produce from turning brown so fast.

The next time you warm canned vegetables such as carrots or green beans, drain and heat the vegetables in ¼ cup beef or chicken broth. It gives a nice variation to an old standby. Here's a simple **white sauce** for vegetables and casseroles without using added fat that can be made by spraying a medium saucepan with butter-flavored cooking spray. Place 1½ cups evaporated skim milk and 3 tablespoons flour in a covered jar. Shake well. Pour into sprayed saucepan and cook over medium heat until thick, stirring constantly. Add salt and pepper to taste. You can also add ½ cup canned drained mushrooms and/or 3 ounces (¾ cup) shredded reduced-fat cheese. Continue cooking until cheese melts.

Zip up canned or frozen green beans with **chunky salsa**: ½ cup to 2 cups beans. Heat thoroughly. Chunky salsa also makes a wonderful dressing on lettuce salads. It only counts as a vegetable, so enjoy.

Another wonderful **South of the Border** dressing can be stirred up by using ½ cup of chunky salsa and ¼ cup fat-free Ranch dressing. Cover and store in your refrigerator. Use as a dressing for salads or as a topping for baked potatoes.

For **gravy** with all the "old time" flavor but without the extra fat, try this almost effortless way to prepare it. (It's almost as easy as opening up a store-bought jar.) Pour the juice off your roasted meat, then set the roast aside to "rest" for about 20 minutes. Place the juice in an uncovered cake pan or other large flat pan (we want the large air surface to speed up the cooling process) and put in the freezer until the fat congeals on top and you can skim it off. Or, if you prefer, use a skimming pitcher purchased at your kitchen gadget store. Either way, measure about 1½ cups skimmed broth and pour into a medium saucepan. Cook over medium heat until heated through, about 5 minutes. In a covered jar, combine ½ cup water or cooled potato broth with 3 tablespoons flour. Shake well. Pour flour mixture into warmed juice. Combine well using a wire whisk. Continue cooking until gravy thickens, about 5 minutes. Season with salt and pepper to taste.

Why did I use flour instead of cornstarch? Because any leftovers will reheat nicely with the flour base and would not with a cornstarch base. Also, 3 tablespoons of flour works out to 1 Bread/Starch exchange. This virtually fat-free gravy makes about 2 cups, so you could spoon about ½ cup gravy on your low-fat mashed potatoes and only have to count your gravy as ¼ Bread/Starch exchange.

Desserts

Thaw **lite whipped topping** in the refrigerator overnight. Never try to force the thawing by stirring or using a microwave to soften. Stirring it will remove the air from the topping that gives it the lightness and texture we want, and there's not enough fat in it to survive being heated.

How can I **frost an entire pie with just ½ cup of whipped topping?** First, don't use an inexpensive brand. I use Cool Whip Lite or La Creme Lite. Make sure the topping is fully thawed. Always spread from the center to the sides using a rubber spatula. This way, ½ cup topping will literally cover an entire pie. Remember, the operative word is *frost*, not pile the entire container on top of the pie!

For a special treat that tastes anything but "diet," try placing **spreadable fruit** in a container and microwave for about 15 seconds. Then pour the melted fruit spread over a serving of nonfat ice cream or frozen yogurt. One tablespoon of spreadable fruit is equal to 1 fruit serving. Some combinations to get you started are apricot over chocolate ice cream, strawberry over strawberry ice cream, or any flavor over vanilla.

Another way I use spreadable fruit is to make a delicious **topping for a cheesecake or angel food cake**. I take ½ cup of fruit and ½ cup Cool Whip Lite and blend the two together with a teaspoon of coconut extract.

Here's a really **good topping** for the fall of the year. Place 1½ cups unsweetened applesauce in a medium saucepan or 4-cup glass measure. Stir in 2 tablespoons raisins, 1 teaspoon apple pie spice, and

2 tablespoons Cary's Sugar Free Maple Syrup. Cook over medium heat on stove or process on HIGH in microwave until warm. Then spoon about ½ cup warm mixture over pancakes, French toast, or fat-free and sugar-free vanilla ice cream. It's as close as you will get to guilt-free apple pie!

A quick yet tasty way to prepare **strawberries for shortcake** is to place about ¾ cup sliced strawberries, 2 tablespoons Diet Mountain Dew, and sugar substitute to equal ¼ cup sugar in a blender container. Process on BLEND until mixture is smooth. Pour mixture into bowl. Add 1¼ cups sliced strawberries and mix well. Cover and refrigerate until ready to serve with shortcake.

The next time you are making treats for the family, try using **unsweetened applesauce** for some or all of the required oil in the recipe. For instance, if the recipe calls for ½ cup cooking oil, use up to the ½ cup in applesauce. It works and most people will not even notice the difference. It's great in purchased cake mixes, but so far I haven't been able to figure out a way to deep-fat fry with it!

Another trick I often use is to include tiny amounts of "real people" food, such as coconut, but extend the flavor by using extracts. Try it—you will be surprised by how little of the real thing you can use and still feel you are not being deprived.

If you are preparing a pie filling that has ample moisture, just line **graham crackers** in the bottom of a 9-by-9-inch cake pan. Pour the filling over the top of the crackers. Cover and refrigerate until the moisture has enough time to soften the crackers. Overnight is best. This eliminates the added **fats and sugars of a piecrust.**

When **stirring fat-free cream cheese to soften it**, use only a sturdy spoon, never an electric mixer. The speed of a mixer can cause the cream cheese to lose its texture and become watery.

Did you know you can make your own **fruit-flavored yogurt?** Mix 1 tablespoon of any flavor of spreadable fruit spread with ¾ cup plain yogurt. It's every bit as tasty and much cheaper. You can also make your own **lemon yogurt** by combining 3 cups plain fat-free yogurt with 1 tub Crystal Light lemonade powder. Mix well, cover, and store in refrigerator. I think you will be pleasantly surprised by the ease, cost, and flavor of this "made from scratch" calcium-rich treat. P.S.: You can make any flavor you like by using any of the Crystal Light mixes—Cranberry? Iced tea? You decide.

Sugar-free puddings and gelatins are important to many of my recipes, but if you prefer to avoid sugar substitutes, you could still prepare the recipes with regular puddings or gelatins. The calories would be higher, but you would still be cooking low-fat.

When a recipe calls for **chopped nuts** (and you only have whole ones), who wants to dirty the food processor just for a couple of tablespoons? You could try to chop them using your cutting board, but be prepared for bits and pieces to fly all over the kitchen. I use "Grandma's food processor." I use the biggest nuts I can find, put them in a small glass bowl, and chop them into chunks just the right size using a metal biscuit cutter.

If you have a **leftover muffin** and are looking for something a little different for breakfast, you can make a "**breakfast sundae.**" Crumble the muffin into a cereal bowl. Sprinkle a serving of fresh fruit over it and top with a couple of tablespoons nonfat plain yogurt sweetened with sugar substitute and your choice of extract. The thought of it just might make you jump out of bed with a smile on your face. (Speaking of muffins, did you know that if you fill the unused muffin wells with water when baking muffins, you help ensure more even baking and protect the muffin pan at the same time?) Another muffin hint: Lightly spray the inside of paper baking cups with butter-flavored cooking spray before spooning the muffin batter into them. Then you won't end up with paper clinging to your fresh-baked muffins.

The secret of making **good meringues** without sugar is to use 1 tablespoon of Sprinkle Sweet or Sugar Twin for every egg white, and a small amount of extract. Use ½ to 1 teaspoon for the batch. Almond, vanilla, and coconut are all good choices. Use the same amount of cream of tartar you usually do. Bake the meringue in the same old way. Don't think you can't have meringue pies because you can't eat sugar. You can, if you do it my way. (Remember that egg whites whip up best at room temperature.)

Homemade or Store-Bought?

I've been asked which is better for you: homemade from scratch, or purchased foods. My answer is *both!* They each have a place in a healthy lifestyle, and what that place is has everything to do with you.

Take **piecrusts**, for instance. If you love spending your spare time in the kitchen preparing foods, and you're using low-fat, low-sugar, and reasonably low sodium ingredients, go for it! But if, like so many people, your time is limited and you've learned to read labels, you could be better off using purchased foods.

I know that when I prepare a pie (and I experiment with a couple of pies each week, because this is Cliff's favorite dessert) I use a purchased crust. Why? Mainly because I can't make a good-tasting piecrust that is lower in fat than the brands I use. Also, purchased piecrusts fit my rule of "If it takes longer to fix than to eat, forget it!"

I've checked the nutrient information for the purchased piecrusts against recipes for traditional and "diet" piecrusts, using my computer software program. The purchased crust calculated lower in both fat and calories! I have tried some low-fat and low-sugar recipes, but they just didn't spark my taste buds, or were so complicated you needed an engineering degree just to get the crust in the pie plate.

I'm very happy with the purchased piecrusts in my recipes, because the finished product rarely, if ever, has more than 30 percent of total calories coming from fats. I also believe that we have to prepare foods our families and friends will eat with us on a regular basis and not feel deprived, or we've wasted time, energy, and money.

I could use a purchased "lite" **pie filling**, but instead I make my own. Here I can save both fat and sugar, and still make the filling almost as fast as opening a can. The bottom line: Know what you have to spend when it comes to both time and fat/sugar calories, then make the best decision you can for you and your family. And don't go without an occasional piece of pie because you think it isn't *necessary*. A delicious pie prepared in a healthy way is one of the simple pleasures of life. It's a little thing, but it can make all the difference between just getting by with the bare minimum and living a full and healthy lifestyle.

Many people have experimented with my tip about **substituting applesauce and artificial sweetener for butter and sugar**, but what if you aren't satisfied with the result? One woman wrote to me about a recipe for her grandmother's cookies that called for 1 cup butter and 1½ cups sugar. Well, any recipe that depends on as much butter and sugar as this one does is generally not a good candidate for "healthy exchanges." The original recipe needed a large quantity of fat to produce a crisp cookie just like Grandma made.

Unsweetened applesauce can be used to substitute for vegetable oil with various degrees of success, but not to replace butter, lard, or margarine. If your recipe calls for ½ cup oil or less, and it's a quick bread, muffin, or bar cookie, it should work to replace the oil with applesauce. If the recipe calls for more than ½ cup oil, then experiment with half oil, half applesauce. You've still made the recipe healthier, even if you haven't removed all the oil from it.

Another rule for healthy substitution: Up to ½ cup sugar or less can be replaced by *an artificial sweetener that can withstand the heat of baking*, like Sugar Twin or Sprinkle Sweet. If it requires more than ½ cup sugar, cut the amount needed by 75 percent and use ½ cup sugar substitute and sugar for the rest. Other options: reduce the butter and sugar by 25 percent and see if the finished product still satisfies you in taste and appearance. Or, make the cookies just like Grandma did, realizing they are part of your family's holiday tradition. Enjoy a moderate serving of a couple of cookies once or twice during the season, and just forget about them the rest of the year.

I'm sure you'll add to this list of cooking tips as you begin preparing Healthy Exchanges recipes and discover how easy it can be to adapt your own favorite recipes using these ideas and your own common sense.

A Peek into My Pantry and My Favorite Brands

Everyone asks me what foods I keep on hand and what brands I use. There are lots of good products on the grocery shelves today—many more than we dreamed about even a year or two ago. And I can't wait to see what's out there twelve months from now. The following are my staples and, where appropriate, my favorites *at this time.* I feel these products are healthier, tastier, easy to get—and deliver the most flavor for the least amount of fat, sugar, or calories. If you find others you like as well *or better,* please use them. This is only a guide to make your grocery shopping and cooking easier.

Fat-free plain yogurt (*Yoplait or Dannon*)
Nonfat dry skim milk powder (*Carnation*)
Evaporated skim milk (*Carnation*)
Skim milk
Fat-free cottage cheese
Fat-free cream cheese (*Philadelphia*)
Fat-free mayonnaise (*Kraft*)
Fat-free salad dressings (*Kraft*)
Fat-free sour cream (*Land O Lakes*)
Reduced-calorie margarine (*Weight Watchers, Promise, or Smart Beat*)
Cooking spray:
    Olive-oil flavored and regular (*Pam*)
    Butter flavored for sautéing (*Weight Watchers*)

Butter flavored for spritzing *after* cooking (*I Can't Believe It's Not Butter!*)

Vegetable oil (*Puritan Canola Oil*)

Reduced-calorie whipped topping (*Cool Whip Lite or Cool Whip Free*)

Sugar Substitute
  if no heating is involved (*Equal*)
  if heating is required
    white (*Sugar Twin or Sprinkle Sweet*)
    brown (*Brown Sugar Twin*)

Sugar-free gelatin and pudding mixes (*JELL-O*)

Baking mix (*Bisquick Reduced Fat*)

Pancake mix (*Aunt Jemima Reduced Calorie*)

Reduced-calorie pancake syrup (*Cary's Sugar Free*)

Parmesan cheese (*Kraft fat-free*)

Reduced-fat cheese (*Kraft ⅓ Less Fat*)

Shredded frozen potatoes (*Mr. Dell's*)

Spreadable fruit spread (*Knott's Berry Farm, Smucker's, or Welch's*)

Peanut butter (*Peter Pan reduced-fat, Jif reduced-fat, or Skippy reduced-fat*)

Chicken broth (*Healthy Request*)

Beef broth (*Swanson*)

Tomato sauce (*Hunt's—Chunky and Regular*)

Canned soups (*Healthy Request*)

Tomato juice (*Campbell's Reduced-Sodium*)

Ketchup (*Heinz Light Harvest or Healthy Choice*)

Purchased piecrust
  unbaked (*Pillsbury—from dairy case*)
  graham cracker, butter flavored, or chocolate flavored (*Keebler*)

Crescent rolls (*Pillsbury Reduced Fat*)

Pastrami and corned beef (*Carl Buddig Lean*)

Luncheon meats (*Healthy Choice or Oscar Mayer*)

Ham (*Dubuque 97% fat-free and reduced-sodium or Healthy Choice*)

Frankfurters and Kielbasa sausage (*Healthy Choice*)

Canned white chicken, packed in water (*Swanson*)

Canned tuna, packed in water (*Chicken of the Sea*)

90 to 95 percent lean ground turkey and beef

Soda crackers (*Nabisco Fat-Free*)
Reduced-calorie bread—40 calories per slice or less
Hamburger buns—80 calories each (*Less*)
Rice—instant, regular, brown, and wild
Instant potato flakes (*Betty Crocker Potato Buds*)
Noodles, spaghetti, and macaroni
Salsa (*Chi Chi's Mild Chunky*)
Pickle relish—dill, sweet, and hot dog
Mustard—Dijon, prepared, and spicy
Unsweetened apple juice
Unsweetened applesauce
Fruit—fresh, frozen (no sugar added), or canned in juice
Vegetables—fresh, frozen, or canned
Spices—JO's Spices
Lemon and lime juice (in small plastic fruit-shaped bottles
    found in produce section)
Instant fruit beverage mixes (*Crystal Light*)
Dry dairy beverage mixes (*Nestlé's Quik and Swiss Miss*)
"Ice Cream"—*Wells' Blue Bunny sugar- and fat-free*

The items on my shopping list are everyday foods found in just about any grocery store in America. But all are as low in fat, sugar, calories, and sodium as I can find—and that still taste good! I can make any recipe in my cookbooks and newsletters as long as I have my cupboards and refrigerator stocked with these items. Whenever I use the last of any one item, I just make sure I pick up another supply the next time I'm at the store.

If your grocer does not stock these items, why not ask if they can be ordered on a trial basis? If the store agrees to do so, be sure to tell your friends to stop by, so that sales are good enough to warrant restocking the new products. Competition for shelf space is fierce, so only products that sell well stay around.

Shopping The Healthy Exchanges Way

Sometimes, as part of a cooking demonstration, I take the group on a field trip to the nearest supermarket. There's no better place to share my discoveries about which healthy products taste best, which are best for you, and which healthy products don't deliver enough taste to include in my recipes.

While I'd certainly enjoy accompanying you to your neighborhood store, we'll have to settle for a field trip *on paper*. I've tasted and tried just about every fat- and sugar-free product on the market, but so many new ones keep coming all the time, you're going to have to learn to play detective on your own. I've turned label reading into an art, but often the label doesn't tell me everything I need to know.

Sometimes you'll find, as I have, that the product with *no* fat doesn't provide the taste satisfaction you require; other times, a no-fat or low-fat product just doesn't cook up the same way as the original product. And some foods, including even the leanest meats, can't eliminate *all* the fat. That's okay, though—a healthy diet should include anywhere from 15 to 25 percent of total calories from fat on any given day.

Take my word for it—your supermarket is filled with lots of delicious foods that can and should be part of your healthy diet for life. Come, join me as we check it out on the way to the checkout!

First stop, the **salad dressing** aisle. Salad dressing is usually a high-fat food, but there are great alternatives available. Let's look first at the regular Ranch dressing—2 tablespoons have 170 calories and

18 grams of fat—and who can eat just 2 tablespoons? Already, that's about half the fat grams most people should consume in a day. Of course, it's the most flavorful too. Now let's look at the low-fat version. Two tablespoons have 110 calories and 11 grams of fat; they took about half of the fat out, but there's still a lot of sugar there. The fat-free version has 50 calories and zero grams of fat, but they also took most of the flavor out. Here's what you do to get it back: add a tablespoon of fat-free mayonnaise, a few more parsley flakes, and about a half teaspoon of sugar substitute to your 2-tablespoon serving. That trick, with the fat-free mayo and sugar substitute, will work with just about any fat-free dressing and give it more of that full-bodied flavor of the high-fat version. Be careful not to add too much sugar substitute—you don't want it to become sickeningly sweet.

I use Kraft fat-free **mayonnaise** at 10 calories per tablespoon to make scalloped potatoes, too. The Smart Beat brand is also a good one.

Before I buy anything at the store, I read the label carefully: the total fat plus the saturated fat; I look to see how many calories are in a realistic serving, and I say to myself, Would I eat that much—or would I eat more? I look at the sodium and I look at the total carbohydrates. I like to check those ingredients because I'm cooking for diabetics and heart patients too. And I check the total calories from fat.

Remember that 1 fat gram equals 9 calories, while 1 protein or 1 carbohydrate gram equals 4 calories.

A wonderful new product is I Can't Believe It's Not Butter! spray, with zero calories and zero grams of fat in four squirts. It's great for your air-popped popcorn. As for **light margarine spread**, beware—most of the fat-free brands don't melt on toast, and they don't taste very good either, so I just leave them on the shelf. For the few times I do use a light margarine I tend to buy Smart Beat Ultra, Promise Ultra, or Weight Watchers Light Ultra. The number-one ingredient in them is water. I occasionally use the light margarine in cooking, but I don't really put margarine on my toast anymore. I use apple butter or make a spread with fat-free cream cheese mixed with a little spreadable fruit instead.

So far, Pillsbury hasn't released a reduced-fat **crescent roll**, so you'll only get one crescent roll per serving from me. I usually make eight of the rolls serve twelve by using them for a crust. The house brands may be lower in fat, but they're usually not as good flavor wise—and don't quite cover the pan when you use them to make a crust. If you're going to use crescent rolls with lots of other stuff on top, then a house brand might be fine.

The Pillsbury French Loaf makes a wonderful **pizza crust** and fills a giant jelly-roll pan. One-fifth of this package "costs" you only 1 gram of fat (and I don't even let you have that much!). Once you use this for your pizza crust, you will never go back to anything else instead. I use it to make calzones too.

I only use Philadelphia fat-free **cream cheese** because it has the best consistency. I've tried other brands, but I wasn't happy with them. Healthy Choice makes lots of great products, but their cream cheese just doesn't work as well with my recipes.

Let's move to the **cheese** aisle. My preferred brand is Kraft ⅓ Less Fat Shredded Cheeses. I will not use the fat-free versions because *they don't melt*. I would gladly give up sugar and fat, but I will not give up flavor. This is a happy compromise. I use the reduced-fat version, I use less, and I use it where your eyes "eat" it, on top of the recipe. So you walk away satisfied and with a finished product that's very low in fat. If you want to make grilled cheese sandwiches for your kids, use the Kraft ⅓ Less Fat cheese slices, and it'll taste exactly like the one they're used to. The fat-free will not.

Some brands have come out with a fat-free **hot dog**, but the ones we've tasted haven't been very good. So far, among the low-fat brands, I think Healthy Choice tastes the best. Did you know that regular hot dogs have as many as 15 grams of fat?

Dubuque's Extra-Lean Reduced-Sodium **ham** tastes wonderful, reduces the sodium as well as the fat, and gives you a larger serving. Don't be fooled by products called turkey ham; they may *not* be lower in fat than a very lean pork product. Here's one label as an example: I checked a brand of turkey ham called Genoa. It gives you a 2-ounce serving for 70 calories and 3½ grams of fat. The Dubuque extra-lean ham, made from pork, gives you a 3-ounce serving for 90 calories, but only 2½ grams of fat. *You get more food and less fat.*

The same can be true for packaged **ground turkey**; if you're not buying *fresh* ground turkey, you may be getting a product with turkey skin and a lot of fat ground up in it. Look to be sure the package is labeled with the fat content; if it isn't, run the other way!

Your best bets in **snack foods** are pretzels, which are always low in fat, as well as the chips from the Guiltless Gourmet, which taste especially good with one of my dips.

Frozen dinners can be expensive and high in sodium, but it's smart to have two or three in the freezer as a backup when your best-laid plans go awry and you need to grab something on the run. But it's not a good idea to rely on them too much—what if you can't get to the store to get them, or you're short on cash? The sodium can be high in some of them because they often replace the fat with salt, so do read the labels. Also ask yourself if the serving is enough to satisfy you; for many of us, it's not.

Egg substitute is expensive, and probably not necessary unless you're cooking for someone who has to worry about every bit of cholesterol in their diet. If you occasionally have a fried egg or an omelet, *use the real egg.* For cooking, you can usually substitute two egg whites for one whole egg. Most of the time it won't make any difference, but check your recipe carefully.

Frozen pizzas aren't particularly healthy, but used occasionally, in moderation, they're okay. Your best bet is to make your own using the Pillsbury French Crust. Take a look at the frozen pizza package of your choice, though, because you may find that plain cheese pizza, which you might think would be the healthiest, might actually have the most fat. Since there's nothing else on there, they have to cover the crust with a heavy layer of high-fat cheese. A veggie pizza generally uses less cheese and more healthy, crunchy vegetables.

Healthy frozen desserts are hard to find except for the Weight Watchers brands. I've always felt that their portions are so small, and for their size still pretty high in fat and sugar. (This is one of the reasons I think I'll be successful marketing my frozen desserts someday. After Cliff tasted one of my earliest healthy pies—and licked the plate clean—he remarked that if I ever opened a restaurant, people would keep coming back for my desserts alone!) Keep an eye out for fat-free or very low-fat frozen yogurt or sorbet products. Even Häagen-Dazs, which makes some of the highest fat content ice cream, now has a fat-free fruit sorbet pop out that's pretty good. I'm sure there will be more before too long.

You have to be realistic: what are you willing to do, and what are you *not* willing to do? Let's take bread, for example. Some people just have to have the real thing—rye bread with caraway seeds or a whole-wheat version with bits of bran in it.

I prefer to use reduced-calorie **bread** because I like a *real* sandwich. This way, I can have two slices of bread and it counts as only one bread/starch exchange.

Do you love **croutons?** Forget the ones from the grocery store—they're extremely high in fat. Instead, take reduced-calorie bread, toast it, give it a quick spray of I Can't Believe It's Not Butter! Spray, and let it dry a bit. Cut the bread in cubes. Then, for an extra-good flavor, put the pieces in a plastic bag with a couple of tablespoons of Kraft House Italian (a reduced-fat Parmesan/Romano cheese blend) and shake them up. You might be surprised just how good they are! Another product that's really good for a crouton—Corn Chex cereal. Sprinkle a few Chex on top of your salad, and I think you'll be pleasantly surprised. I've also found that Rice Chex, crushed up, with parsley flakes and a little bit of Parmesan cheese, makes a great topping for casseroles that you used to put potato chips on.

Salad toppers can make a lot of difference in how content you feel after you've eaten. Some low-fat cheese, some homemade croutons, and even some bacon bits on top of your greens deliver an abundance of tasty satisfaction. I always use the real Hormel **bacon bits** instead of the imitation bacon-flavored bits. I only use a small amount, but you get that real bacon flavor—and less fat too.

How I Shop for Myself

I always keep my kitchen stocked with my basic staples; that way, I can go to the cupboard and create new recipes any time I'm inspired. I hope you will take the time (and allot the money) to stock your cupboards with items from the staples list, so you can enjoy developing your own healthy versions of family favorites without making extra trips to the market.

I'm always on the lookout for new products sitting on the grocery shelf. When I spot something I haven't seen before, I'll usually grab it, glance at the front, then turn it around and read the label carefully. I call it looking at the promises (the "come-on" on the front of the package) and then at the warranty (the ingredients list and the label on the back).

If it looks as good on the back as it does on the front, I'll say okay and either create a recipe on the spot or take it home for when I do think of something to do with it. Picking up a new product is just about the only time I buy something not on my list.

The items on my shopping list are normal, everyday foods, but as low-fat and low-sugar (*while still tasting good*) as I can find. I can make any recipe in this book as long as these staples are on my shelves. After using these products for a couple of weeks, you will find it becomes routine to have them on hand. And I promise you, I really don't spend any more at the store now than I did a few years ago when I told myself I couldn't afford some of these items. Back then, of course, plenty of unhealthy, high-priced snacks I really didn't need somehow made the magic leap from the grocery shelves into my cart. Who was I kidding?

Yes, you often have to pay a little more for fat-free or low-fat products, including meats. But since I frequently use a half pound of meat to serve four to six people, your cost per serving will be much lower.

Try adding up what you were spending before on chips and cookies, premium brand ice cream and fatty cuts of meat, and you'll soon see that we've *streamlined* your shopping cart, and taken the weight off your pocketbook as well as your hips!

Remember, your good health is *your* business—but it's big business too. Write to the manufacturers of products you and your family enjoy but feel are just too high in fat, sugar, or sodium to be part of your new healthy lifestyle. Companies are spending millions of dollars to respond to consumers' concerns about food products, and I bet that in the next few years, you'll discover fat-free and low-fat versions of nearly every product piled high on your supermarket shelves!

The Healthy Exchanges Kitchen

You might be surprised to discover I still don't have a massive test kitchen stocked with every modern appliance and handy gadget ever made. The tiny galley kitchen where I first launched Healthy Exchanges has room for only one person at a time, but it never stopped me from feeling the sky's the limit when it comes to seeking out great healthy taste!

Because storage is at such a premium in my kitchen, I don't waste space with equipment I don't really need. Here's a list of what I consider worth having. If you notice serious gaps in your equipment, you can probably find most of what you need at a local discount store or garage sale. If your kitchen is equipped with more sophisticated appliances, don't feel guilty about using them. Enjoy every appliance you can find room for or that you can afford. Just be assured that healthy, quick, and delicious food can be prepared with the "basics."

A Healthy Exchanges Kitchen Equipment List

Good-quality nonstick skillets (medium, large)
Good-quality saucepans (small, medium, large)
Glass mixing bowls (small, medium, large)
Glass measures (1-cup, 2-cup, 4-cup, 8-cup)

Sharp knives (paring, chef, butcher)
Rubber spatulas
Wire whisks
Measuring spoons
Measuring cups
Large mixing spoons
Egg separator
Covered jar
Vegetable parer
Grater
Potato masher
Electric mixer
Electric blender
Electric skillet
4-inch round custard dishes
Glass pie plates
8-by-8-inch glass baking dishes
Cake pans (9-by-9, 9-by-13-inch)
10¾-by-7-by-1½-inch biscuit pan
Cookie sheets (good nonstick ones)
Jelly-roll pan
Muffin tins
5-by-9-inch bread pan
Plastic colander
Cutting board
Pie wedge server
Cooking timer
Slow cooker
Air popper for popcorn
Kitchen scales (unless you *always* use my recipes)
Wire racks for cooling baked goods
Electric toaster oven (to conserve energy for those times when
    only one item is being baked or for a recipe that requires a
    short baking time)
Square-shaped server
Can opener (I prefer manual)
Rolling pin

How to Read a Healthy Exchanges® Recipe

The Healthy Exchanges Nutritional Analysis

Before using these recipes you may wish to consult your physician or health-care provider to be sure they are appropriate for you. The information in this book is not intended to take the place of any medical advice. It reflects my experiences, studies, research, and opinions regarding healthy eating.

Each recipe includes nutritional information calculated in three ways:

Healthy Exchanges Weight Loss Choices™ or Exchanges
Calories, fiber, and fat grams
Diabetic exchanges

In every Healthy Exchanges recipe, the diabetic exchanges have been calculated by a Registered Dietitian. All the other calculations were done by computer, using the Food Processor II software. When the ingredient listing gives more than one choice, the first ingredient listed is the one used in the recipe analysis. Due to inevitable variations in the ingredients you choose to use, the nutritional values should be considered approximate.

The annotation "(limited)" following Protein counts in some recipes indicates that consumption of whole eggs should be limited to four per week.

Please note the following symbols:

☆This star means read the recipe's directions carefully for special instructions about **division** of ingredients.

❋ This symbol indicates **FREEZES WELL**.

A Few Cooking Terms to Ease the Way

Everyone can learn to cook *The Healthy Exchanges Way*. It's simple, it's quick, and the results are delicious! If you've tended to avoid the kitchen because you find recipe instructions confusing or complicated, I hope I can help you feel more confident. I'm not offering a full cooking course here, just some terms I use often that I know you'll want to understand.

Bake: To cook food in the oven; sometimes called roasting

Beat: To mix very fast with a spoon, wire whisk, or electric mixer

Blend: To mix two or more ingredients together thoroughly so that the mixture is smooth

Boil: To cook in liquid until bubbles form

Brown: To cook at low to medium-low heat until ingredients turn brown

Chop: To cut food into small pieces with a knife, blender, or food processor

Cool: To let stand at room temperature until food is no longer hot to the touch

Combine: To mix ingredients together with a spoon

Dice: To chop into small, even-sized pieces

Drain: To pour off liquid; sometimes you will need to reserve the liquid to use in the recipe, so please read carefully.

Drizzle: To sprinkle drops of liquid (for example, chocolate syrup) lightly over top of food

Fold in: To combine delicate ingredients with other foods by using a gentle, circular motion. Example: adding Cool Whip Lite to an already stirred-up bowl of pudding.

Preheat: To heat your oven to the desired temperature, usually about 10 minutes before you put your food in to bake

Sauté: To cook in skillet or frying pan until food is soft

Simmer: To cook in a small amount of liquid over low heat; this lets the flavors blend without too much liquid evaporating.

Whisk: To beat with a wire whisk until mixture is well mixed; don't worry about finesse here, just use some elbow grease!

How to Measure

I try to make it as easy as possible by providing more than one measurement for many ingredients in my recipes—both the weight in ounces and the amount measured by a measuring cup, for example. Just remember:

- You measure **solids** (flour, Cool Whip Lite, yogurt, macaroni, nonfat dry milk powder) in your set of separate measuring cups (¼, ⅓, ½, 1 cup)

- You measure **liquids** (Diet Mountain Dew, water, tomato juice) in the clear glass or plastic measuring cups that measure ounces, cups, and pints. Set the cup on a level surface and pour the liquid into it, or you may get too much.

- You can use your measuring spoon set for liquids or solids. **Note:** Don't pour a liquid like an extract into a measuring spoon held over the bowl in case you overpour; instead, do it over the sink.

Here are a few handy equivalents:

3 teaspoons	equals	1 tablespoon
4 tablespoons	equals	1/4 cup
5 1/3 tablespoons	equals	1/3 cup
8 tablespoons	equals	1/2 cup
10 2/3 tablespoons	equals	2/3 cup
12 tablespoons	equals	3/4 cup
16 tablespoons	equals	1 cup
2 cups	equals	1 pint
4 cups	equals	1 quart
8 ounces liquid	equals	1 fluid cup

That's it. Now, ready, set, cook!

Soups

My grandma was famous for her wonderful, heartwarming soups that bubbled away for hours on her old-fashioned wood-burning cookstove. What a delicious aroma always filled her kitchen on the days she made soup out of all the good things from her garden, plus fresh meats and homemade stocks. On wintry days when I felt as if nothing could ever make me feel warm again, a bowl of Grandma's soup worked miracles, warming me inside and out!

But few of us have the time anymore to make soup that cooks all day, that uses only ingredients we've personally chopped and diced, or herbs we grew ourselves. Does that mean letting go of the cozy tradition of soups that make us feel oh-so-good? *Not a chance!*

This section brims with easy-to-fix soups made of simple-to-find ingredients, and each one will soon become a family favorite. Who could resist a hearty bowl of Ham Chowder or my Creamy Potato Soup with Cheese Dumplings that taste like the ones Grandma used to make—but serve up so quick you'll be delightfully surprised. Show your loved ones just how much you care—and make soup!

Soups

Creamy Potato Soup with Cheese Dumplings

Oh, could there be a more heartwarming, tummy-pleasing dish than this rich soup, which is made even more wonderful with my easy-to-fix dumplings! It's so satisfying, so cozy and old-fashioned, it'll definitely soothe the soul!   ☻   Serves 4

1½ cups water
2 cups (10 ounces) diced raw potatoes
½ cup chopped onion
1 cup chopped celery
1½ cups (one 12-fluid-ounce can) Carnation Evaporated Skim Milk
¼ teaspoon lemon pepper
6 tablespoons Bisquick Reduced Fat Baking Mix
1 teaspoon dried parsley flakes
3 tablespoons (¾ ounce) shredded Kraft reduced-fat Cheddar cheese
¼ cup skim milk

In a large saucepan, combine water, potatoes, onion, and celery. Bring mixture to a boil. Lower heat, cover, and simmer for 15 minutes or until vegetables are tender. Stir in evaporated skim milk and lemon pepper. In a small bowl, combine baking mix, parsley flakes, and Cheddar cheese. Add skim milk. Mix gently to combine. Drop by tablespoon into hot mixture to form 4 dumplings. Cover and continue simmering for 10 minutes or until dumplings are firm. For each serving, place 1 dumpling into a bowl and spoon about 1 cup of soup over top. Serve at once.

Each serving equals:

HE: 1 Bread • ¾ Vegetable • ¾ Skim Milk • ¼ Protein • 6 Optional Calories

194 Calories • 2 gm Fat • 12 gm Protein • 32 gm Carbohydrate • 328 mg Sodium • 366 mg Calcium • 2 gm Fiber

DIABETIC: 2 Starch/Carbohydrate • ½ Skim Milk

Tomato Basil Corn Soup

This delectably fragrant soup may not cook as long as Grandma's did, but it tastes like the kind that used to be ladled out of a big iron pot. You can enjoy a big bowl of this for so very few calories, you could afford to have "seconds," but you won't have any room left!

○ Serves 4 (1¼ cups)

> 1 (10¾-ounce) can Healthy Request Tomato Soup
> 1 ¾ cups (one 15-ounce can) Hunt's Chunky Tomato Sauce
> 1 cup water
> 2 tablespoons dried onion flakes
> 1 teaspoon dried parsley flakes
> 1 teaspoon dried basil
> 1½ cups frozen whole-kernel corn, thawed

In a medium saucepan, combine tomato soup, tomato sauce, and water. Stir in onion flakes, parsley flakes, and basil. Bring mixture to a boil. Add corn. Mix well to combine. Lower heat and simmer for 10 minutes or until mixture is heated through, stirring occasionally.

HINT: Thaw corn by placing in a colander and rinsing under hot water for one minute.

Each serving equals:

HE: 1¾ Vegetable • ¾ Bread • ½ Slider •
5 Optional Calories

---

149 Calories • 1 gm Fat • 4 gm Protein •
31 gm Carbohydrate • 882 mg Sodium •
38 mg Calcium • 4 gm Fiber

DIABETIC: 2 Vegetable • 1 Starch/Carbohydrate

Reuben Soup

Instead of soup and a favorite deli sandwich, why not try this splendid sandwich-in-a-soup? It's so jam-packed with meat and potatoes, it'll please your husband so much he'll volunteer to clean out the garage without being asked! ❂   Serves 4 (1 cup)

> 1 (10¾-ounce) can Healthy Request Cream of Mushroom Soup
> 1⅓ cups skim milk
> 4 (¾-ounce) slices Kraft reduced-fat Swiss cheese, shredded
> 1⅓ cups (5 ounces) shredded loose packed frozen potatoes
> 1 (2.5-ounce) package Carl Buddig corned beef, shredded
> 1 cup (one 8-ounce can) sauerkraut, well drained and chopped
> 2 slices reduced-calorie rye bread, toasted and cubed

In a medium saucepan, combine mushroom soup, skim milk, and Swiss cheese. Cook over medium heat until cheese melts, stirring often. Stir in potatoes, corned beef, and sauerkraut. Mix well to combine. Lower heat and simmer for 10 minutes, stirring occasionally. When serving, evenly top each bowl with toasted bread cubes.

HINT: Mr. Dell's frozen shredded potatoes are a good choice for this recipe, or raw shredded potatoes may be used in place of frozen potatoes.

Each serving equals:

HE: 1⅔ Protein • ½ Bread • ⅓ Skim Milk •
¼ Vegetable • ½ Slider • 1 Optional Calorie

201 Calories • 4 gm Fat • 15 gm Protein •
24 gm Carbohydrate • 1070 mg Sodium •
381 mg Calcium • 2 gm Fiber

DIABETIC: 1½ Meat • 1½ Starch/Carbohydrate •
½ Vegetable

Old-Fashioned Russian Borscht ❄

No one knows more about making soup to warm you all the way through than the Russian grandmas who serve steaming bowls of this beloved beet soup! Even if you've never been much of a fan of beets on their own, give this rosy-colored soup a try. It's luscious, it's unbelievably low in calories and fat, and it's tasty enough to heat up a winter in Siberia!　　☻　　Serves 4 (1½ cups)

> ½ cup finely chopped onion
> 2 cups (one 16-ounce can) diced beets, undrained
> 1 teaspoon lemon juice
> 3½ cups (two 14½-ounce cans) Swanson Beef Broth
> ½ teaspoon caraway seed
> ¼ cup Land O Lakes no-fat sour cream

In a large saucepan sprayed with butter-flavored cooking spray, sauté onion for 5 minutes or until tender. Stir in undrained beets, lemon juice, beef broth, and caraway seed. Lower heat and simmer for 15 minutes, stirring occasionally. When serving, top each bowl with 1 tablespoon sour cream.

HINT:　If you can't find diced canned beets, purchase canned sliced beets and insert a sharp knife in can or jar and coarsely chop.

Each serving equals:

HE: 1¼ Vegetable • ¼ Slider • 11 Optional Calories

65 Calories • 1 gm Fat • 3 gm Protein •
11 gm Carbohydrate • 971 mg Sodium • 35 mg Calcium •
2 gm Fiber

DIABETIC: 1 Vegetable • ½ Starch/Carbohydrate

Calico Chicken Cabbage Soup ❄

Don't you just love a soup that's so full of meat, veggies, and noodles you could almost eat it with a fork? This old-timey blend needs almost no watching as it simmers, so you can relax before serving dinner to the family!   ☻   Serves 6 (1½ cups)

> *4 cups (two 16-ounce cans) Healthy Request Chicken Broth*
> *1½ cups (8 ounces) diced cooked chicken breast*
> *3 cups finely shredded cabbage*
> *1 cup finely shredded carrots*
> *½ cup diced onion*
> *½ cup diced celery*
> *1 scant cup (1½ ounces) uncooked noodles*
> *1 tablespoon reduced-sodium soy sauce*
> *⅛ teaspoon black pepper*
> *1 teaspoon dried parsley flakes*

In a large saucepan, combine chicken broth, chicken, cabbage, carrots, onion, and celery. Bring mixture to a boil. Add uncooked noodles, soy sauce, black pepper, and parsley flakes. Mix well to combine. Lower heat, cover, and simmer for 20 minutes or until vegetables and noodles are tender, stirring occasionally.

HINT: If you don't have leftovers, purchase a chunk of cooked chicken breast from your local deli.

Each serving equals:

> HE: 1⅔ Vegetable • 1⅓ Protein • ⅓ Bread •
> 11 Optional Calories
>
> ---
>
> 126 Calories • 2 gm Fat • 16 gm Protein •
> 11 gm Carbohydrate • 447 mg Sodium •
> 28 mg Calcium • 1 gm Fiber
>
> ---
>
> DIABETIC: 1 Meat • 1 Vegetable • ½ Starch

Wild Rice and Chicken Soup ❄

Wild rice has always seemed like a luxury, a special treat served only to company on special occasions, but now that it's widely available and well priced, you can stir it into a favorite chicken soup recipe like this one—and feel like "company" in your own home!

❂ Serves 4 (1½ cups)

> 4 cups (two 16-ounce cans) Healthy Request Chicken Broth
> ½ cup chopped onion
> 1 cup shredded carrots
> 1 cup sliced celery
> 1 full cup (6 ounces) diced cooked chicken breast
> 1 (10¾-ounce) can Healthy Request Cream of Mushroom Soup
> 1 scant cup (3 ounces) uncooked instant long-grain and wild rice

In a large saucepan, combine chicken broth, onion, carrots, and celery. Bring mixture to a boil. Add chicken. Mix well to combine. Lower heat, cover, and simmer for 10 minutes or until vegetables are tender, stirring occasionally. Stir in mushroom soup and uncooked rice. Cover and continue simmering for 15 minutes, stirring occasionally.

HINT: If you don't have leftovers, purchase a chunk of cooked chicken breast from your local deli.

Each serving equals:

HE: 1½ Protein • 1¼ Vegetable • ¾ Bread • ½ Slider • 17 Optional Calories

---

187 Calories • 3 gm Fat • 18 gm Protein • 22 gm Carbohydrate • 849 mg Sodium • 83 mg Calcium • 2 gm Fiber

---

DIABETIC: 1½ Meat

Chilly Weather Chili

Traditional chili usually cooked for hours and required lots of efforts from the cook, whoever she (or he) was. Now I've found a way to deliver that classic hearty flavor in minutes instead of hours, and it's so good, your family will smile the way Grandpa did when Grandma brought her special chili to the table! ☻ Serves 6 (1⅔ cups)

> 12 ounces ground 90% lean turkey or beef
> ¾ cup chopped onion
> 1 (10¾-ounce) can Healthy Request Tomato Soup
> 1¾ cups (one 14½-ounce can) stewed tomatoes, undrained
> 10 ounces (one 16-ounce can) red kidney beans, rinsed and drained
> 3½ cups Healthy Request Tomato Juice or any reduced-sodium
>   tomato juice
> 1 tablespoon chili seasoning
> ½ teaspoon paprika
> 1 cup (2¼ ounces) uncooked elbow macaroni

In a large saucepan sprayed with olive oil–flavored cooking spray, brown meat and onion. Add tomato soup, undrained stewed tomatoes, kidney beans, and tomato juice. Mix well to combine. Stir in chili seasoning, paprika, and uncooked macaroni. Bring mixture to a boil. Lower heat and simmer for 20 minutes or until macaroni is tender, stirring occasionally.

Each serving equals:

HE: 2⅓ Protein • 2 Vegetable • ½ Bread • ¼ Slider • 10 Optional Calories

257 Calories • 5 gm Fat • 17 gm Protein • 36 gm Carbohydrate • 512 mg Sodium • 71 mg Calcium • 5 gm Fiber

DIABETIC: 2 Meat • 2 Vegetable • 1½ Starch

Grandma's Basil Vegetable Beef Soup

It used to take the expert hand of an experienced cook to season dishes just right, but even if your grandma never taught you her secret to great vegetable beef soup, I'm happy to share mine! This is a truly filling dish and a wonderful way to use up leftover roast beef if you happen to have any.   ☺   Serves 4 (full 1½ cups)

> 1½ cups (8 ounces) diced cooked lean roast beef
> 2½ cups water
> 1¾ cups (one 14½-ounce can) Swanson Beef Broth
> 2 cups sliced carrots
> ½ cup chopped onion
> 1 teaspoon dried basil
> ¼ teaspoon black pepper
> 2 cups (10 ounces) diced raw potatoes
> 3 cups thinly sliced cabbage

In a large saucepan, combine roast beef, water, beef broth, carrots, onion, basil, and black pepper. Bring mixture to a boil. Add potatoes and cabbage. Mix well to combine. Lower heat, cover, and simmer for 30 minutes, or until vegetables are tender, stirring occasionally.

HINT: If you don't have leftovers, purchase a chunk of lean cooked roast beef from your local deli *or* use Healthy Choice Deli slices.

Each serving equals:

> HE: 2¾ Vegetable • 2 Protein • ½ Bread •
> 8 Optional Calories
> _____
> 205 Calories • 5 gm Fat • 20 gm Protein •
> 20 gm Carbohydrate • 428 mg Sodium • 51 mg Calcium •
> 4 gm Fiber
> _____
> DIABETIC: 2 Meat • 1 Vegetable • 1 Starch

Homestead Vegetable Beef Soup ❄

Doesn't a big spoonful of noodles just say "old-fashioned" without words? Here's a recipe that gives those homey noodles a tasty setting— beefy broth, chunks of veggies, and just enough seasoning to bring it to mouth-pleasing life!   ☻   Serves 4 (1½ cups)

2¾ cups water
1¾ cups (one 14½-ounce can) Swanson Beef Broth
1½ cups (8 ounces) diced cooked lean roast beef
3 cups sliced carrots
1 cup chopped celery
½ cup chopped onion
¼ teaspoon black pepper
¼ teaspoon dried minced garlic
1 teaspoon dried parsley flakes
2 cups (3 ounces) uncooked noodles

In a large saucepan, combine water, beef broth, roast beef, carrots, celery, onion, black pepper, garlic, and parsley flakes. Bring mixture to a boil. Lower heat, cover, and simmer for 20 minutes. Stir in uncooked noodles. Continue simmering for about 15 minutes or until vegetables and noodles are tender, stirring occasionally.

HINT: If you don't have leftovers, purchase a chunk of cooked lean roast beef from your local deli.

Each serving equals:

HE: 2¼ Vegetable • 2 Protein • 1 Bread •
8 Optional Calories

268 Calories • 6 gm Fat • 23 gm Protein •
30 gm Carbohydrate • 533 mg Sodium • 58 mg Calcium •
4 gm Fiber

DIABETIC: 2 Meat • 2 Starch • 1 Vegetable

Ham Chowder

No self-respecting "grandma" would provide a selection of soups without including a chowder like this scrumptious bowl of goodness! You get so much nutrition in one big bowl, you're ready to face the world—or the foot of snow blocking your driveway!   ☻   Serves 4 (1½ cups)

1½ cups (8 ounces) diced raw potatoes

1 cup diced celery

½ cup diced onion

1 cup water

3 tablespoons all-purpose flour

4 cups skim milk ☆

1 full cup (6 ounces) diced Dubuque 97% fat-free ham or any extra-lean ham

1 cup frozen whole-kernel corn, thawed

¼ teaspoon black pepper

¾ cup (3 ounces) shredded Kraft reduced-fat Cheddar cheese

In a large saucepan, combine potatoes, celery, onion, and water. Bring mixture to a boil. Lower heat and simmer 15 minutes or until vegetables are tender. DO NOT DRAIN. In a covered jar, combine flour and 1 cup skim milk. Shake well to blend. Pour milk mixture into saucepan with vegetables. Add remaining 3 cups skim milk, ham, corn, and black pepper. Mix well to combine. Stir in Cheddar cheese and continue simmering for 15 minutes or until cheese melts and mixture thickens, stirring often.

Each serving equals:

HE: 2 Protein • 1¼ Bread • ¾ Skim Milk •
¾ Vegetable

---

285 Calories • 5 gm Fat • 24 gm Protein •
36 gm Carbohydrate • 696 mg Sodium •
462 mg Calcium • 2 gm Fiber

DIABETIC: 1½ Starch • 1½ Meat • 1 Skim Milk •
½ Vegetable

Savory Salads

There are always terrific main dishes at any family potluck, but somehow it's those delectable salads everybody brings that you heap your plate with and always remember! What's a Fourth of July picnic without potato salad and coleslaw, and what better way to gobble down all those healthy servings of vegetables you know you need than to enjoy a fresh and colorful lettuce salad or a crunchy mound of chopped veggies dressed with a flavorful sauce?

I'll never forget sitting at Grandma's table with the boarders and watching their eyes light up as they passed bowls of her savory salads from hand to hand. She might scold them for taking so much they wouldn't have room for the main dish, but she'd smile at their enthusiasm for her tasty food.

This section features the best of my Grandma-style salads, including my Calico Potato Salad (that just sparkles with the colors of her garden) and such yummy and unusual dishes as Macaroni and Cheese Salad and Pineapple Cashew Slaw. Bring these along to your next holiday gathering, and don't be surprised if your bowl is the first to be emptied!

Savory Salads

Festive Carrot Salad

This sweet and crunchy combo looks so pretty on the plate, it's a must for every family reunion . . . and a winner when it's time for your annual company picnic! Kids have always loved carrot salad, and this one, with its extra touch of coconut, makes them smile with every bite. ❂ Serves 4 (¾ cup)

> 1 cup (one 8-ounce can) crushed pineapple, packed in fruit juice, drained, and 2 tablespoons liquid reserved
> 3 cups shredded carrots
> 2 teaspoons flaked coconut
> Sugar substitute to equal 1 tablespoon sugar
> ¼ cup Kraft fat-free mayonnaise

In a medium bowl, combine pineapple, carrots, coconut, and sugar substitute. In a small bowl, combine mayonnaise and reserved pineapple juice. Add mayonnaise mixture to pineapple mixture. Mix well to combine. Refrigerate for at least 30 minutes. Gently stir again just before serving.

Each serving equals:

HE: 1½ Vegetable • ½ Fruit • 14 Optional Calories

80 Calories • 0 gm Fat • 1 gm Protein •
19 gm Carbohydrate • 179 mg Sodium •
36 mg Calcium • 2 gm Fiber

DIABETIC: 2 Vegetable • ½ Fruit

French Green Bean Salad

If green beans are your husband's most-loved vegetables (they're Cliff's, too!), here's another tasty way to serve them! Cliff likes the little bits of onion and the tanginess of the cheese and French dressing, but most of all, he LOVES those beans!   ♥   Serves 4 (¾ cup)

> 4 cups (two 16-ounce cans) French-style green beans, rinsed and
> drained
> 2 teaspoons dried onion flakes
> ⅓ cup Kraft Fat Free French Dressing
> 3 tablespoons (¾ ounce) shredded Kraft reduced-fat Cheddar cheese

In a medium bowl, combine green beans, onion flakes, and French dressing. Cover and refrigerate for at least 2 hours. Just before serving, stir in Cheddar cheese.

Each serving equals:

HE: 2 Vegetable • ¼ Protein • ¼ Slider •
13 Optional Calories

77 Calories • 1 gm Fat • 2 gm Protein •
15 gm Carbohydrate • 245 mg Sodium •
72 mg Calcium • 2 gm Fiber

DIABETIC: 2 Vegetable • ½ Starch/Carbohydrate

Onion-Cucumber Salad

This cool and crunchy salad makes a perfect side dish when you're serving an old-fashioned meat loaf supper. Its color and texture is a real palate pleaser, and the vinegar-based dressing just tickles your taste buds! ☻ Serves 4 (½ cup)

2 cups thinly sliced unpeeled cucumber
½ cup thinly sliced onion
½ cup white vinegar
½ cup water
Sugar substitute to equal 2 tablespoons sugar
1 teaspoon dried parsley flakes
⅛ teaspoon black pepper

In a large bowl, combine cucumber and onion. In a small bowl, combine vinegar, water, sugar substitute, parsley flakes, and black pepper. Pour dressing mixture over cucumber mixture. Cover and refrigerate for at least 1 hour. Just before serving, drain vegetables.

Each serving equals:

HE: 1¼ Vegetable • 3 Optional Calories

20 Calories • 0 gm Fat • 0 gm Protein •
5 gm Carbohydrate • 133 mg Sodium • 15 mg Calcium •
1 gm Fiber

DIABETIC: 1 Free Food

Creamy Garden Delight Salad

When Grandma's garden was at its ripe and beautiful best, this is just the kind of salad she stirred up to show off its bounty! It's pretty and crisp, the kind of salad every Midwestern table features in midsummer. ☻ Serves 8 (¾ cup)

3 cups coarsely chopped fresh tomatoes
1 cup diced unpeeled cucumbers
½ cup chopped onion
½ cup chopped green bell pepper
½ cup Kraft Fat Free Ranch Dressing
¼ cup Kraft fat-free mayonnaise

In a medium bowl, combine tomatoes, cucumbers, onion, and green pepper. Add Ranch dressing and mayonnaise. Mix gently to combine. Cover and refrigerate for at least 30 minutes. Gently stir again just before serving.

Each serving equals:

HE: 1¼ Vegetable • ¼ Slider • 8 Optional Calories

48 Calories • 0 gm Fat • 1 gm Protein •
11 gm Carbohydrate • 232 mg Sodium • 9 mg Calcium •
1 gm Fiber

DIABETIC: 2 Vegetable

Country Coleslaw

If you're used to classic coleslaw with the same old dressing all the time, I hope you'll be adventurous and give this combo a chance. That uniquely nutty flavor provided by the peanut butter performs a kind of culinary magic that will make your family say "Abracadabra!"

⏾ Serves 6 (⅔ cup)

4¼ cups purchased coleslaw mix
2 tablespoons diced onion
2 tablespoons diced green bell pepper
½ cup Kraft fat-free mayonnaise
3 tablespoons Peter Pan reduced-fat peanut butter (creamy or
    chunky)
Sugar substitute to equal 2 teaspoons sugar
1 teaspoon cider vinegar

In a large bowl, combine coleslaw mix, onion, and green pepper. In a small bowl, combine mayonnaise, peanut butter, sugar substitute, and vinegar. Add dressing mixture to vegetable mixture. Mix well to combine. Cover and refrigerate for at least 30 minutes. Gently stir again just before serving.

HINT: 3¼ cups shredded cabbage and 1 cup shredded carrots
    may be used in place of purchased coleslaw mix.

Each serving equals:

HE: 1½ Vegetable • ½ Protein • ½ Fat •
14 Optional Calories

74 Calories • 3 gm Fat • 2 gm Protein •
11 gm Carbohydrate • 313 mg Sodium •
22 mg Calcium • 2 gm Fiber

DIABETIC: 1 Vegetable • ½ Starch/Carbohydrate • ½ Fat

Pineapple Cashew Slaw

Cashews in a healthy recipe? you may ask in disbelief . . . Why not, this grandma replies with a grin! I've learned how to use small amounts of formerly "off-limits" real-life foods to make my good-for-you dishes really, really good!   ❂   Serves 6 (⅔ cup)

> 4 cups purchased coleslaw mix
> 1 cup (one 8-ounce can) pineapple tidbits, packed in fruit juice,
>   drained, and 2 tablespoons liquid reserved
> ¼ cup (1 ounce) chopped cashews
> ½ cup Kraft fat-free mayonnaise
> ¼ cup Land O Lakes no-fat sour cream
> Sugar substitute to equal 2 teaspoons sugar

In a large bowl, combine coleslaw mix, pineapple, and cashews. In a small bowl, combine mayonnaise, sour cream, sugar substitute, and reserved pineapple juice. Add mayonnaise mixture to coleslaw mixture. Mix gently to combine. Cover and refrigerate for at least 30 minutes. Gently stir again just before serving.

HINTS: 1. If you can't find pineapple tidbits, use pineapple chunks and coarsely chop.

              2. 3 cups shredded cabbage and 1 cup shredded carrots may be used in place of purchased coleslaw mix.

Each serving equals:

HE: 1⅓ Vegetable • ⅓ Fruit • ⅓ Fat • ¼ Slider • 14 Optional Calories

---

94 Calories • 2 gm Fat • 2 gm Protein • 17 gm Carbohydrate • 236 mg Sodium • 40 mg Calcium • 2 gm Fiber

---

DIABETIC: 1 Vegetable • 1 Starch/Carbohydrate

Calico Potato Salad

I like food to be colorful as well as tasty, and this picnic-perfect potato salad is pretty as a picture! Every grandma has her own wonderful combination of flavors for this family favorite, and this is one my own family cheered when I served it.   ☮   Serves 6 (⅔ cup)

3 full cups (16 ounces) diced cooked potatoes
½ cup diced unpeeled cucumber
¼ cup chopped onion
¼ cup chopped green bell pepper
¼ cup (one 2-ounce jar) diced pimiento, drained
½ cup Kraft fat-free mayonnaise
Sugar substitute to equal 2 teaspoons sugar
1 tablespoon white vinegar
1 teaspoon prepared mustard
⅛ teaspoon black pepper
2 hard-boiled eggs, coarsely chopped

In a large bowl, combine potatoes, cucumber, onion, green pepper, and pimiento. In a small bowl, combine mayonnaise, sugar substitute, vinegar, mustard, and black pepper. Add dressing mixture to potato mixture. Mix well to combine. Gently fold in eggs. Cover and refrigerate for at least 30 minutes. Gently stir again just before serving.

HINT: If you want the look and feel of eggs without the cholesterol, toss out the yolk and dice the whites.

Each serving equals:

HE: ⅔ Bread • ⅓ Protein (limited) • ⅓ Vegetable •
14 Optional Calories

78 Calories • 2 gm Fat • 3 gm Protein •
12 gm Carbohydrate • 187 mg Sodium •
18 mg Calcium • 1 gm Fiber

DIABETIC: 1 Starch/Carbohydrate

Macaroni and Cheese Salad

If your kids could eat macaroni and cheese three times a day, I'm happy to suggest a super salad that celebrates this down-home country classic! With so much flavor in every bite, this dish is a great choice for your next potluck or buffet party.   ❂   Serves 4 (1 cup)

> 2 cups cold cooked elbow macaroni, rinsed and drained
> 3/4 cup (3 ounces) shredded Kraft reduced-fat Cheddar cheese
> 1 cup diced celery
> 1 cup coarsely chopped fresh tomatoes
> 1/4 cup diced onion
> 1/4 cup diced green bell pepper
> 1/2 cup Kraft Fat Free Ranch Dressing
> 1/3 cup Kraft fat-free mayonnaise
> 1 teaspoon prepared mustard
> 1/4 teaspoon black pepper

In a large bowl, combine macaroni, Cheddar cheese, celery, tomatoes, onion, and green pepper. Add Ranch dressing, mayonnaise, mustard, and black pepper. Mix gently to combine. Cover and refrigerate for at least 30 minutes. Gently stir again just before serving.

HINT: 1 1/3 cups uncooked elbow macaroni usually cooks to about 2 cups.

Each serving equals:

> HE: 1 1/4 Vegetable • 1 Bread • 1 Protein • 3/4 Slider • 3 Optional Calories
>
> 228 Calories • 4 gm Fat • 10 gm Protein • 38 gm Carbohydrate • 549 mg Sodium • 175 mg Calcium • 2 gm Fiber
>
> DIABETIC: 2 Starch/Carbohydrate • 1 Meat • 1/2 Vegetable

Three Bean Salad

I think Grandma considered her three bean salad the ultimate man-pleaser, but all the women in our house have always loved it too! If tradition and old-time values could be spooned up in a savory salad, this would be it! ☻ Serves 8 (¾ cup)

> 2 cups (one 16-ounce can) cut green beans, rinsed and drained
> 2 cups (one 16-ounce can) cut wax beans, rinsed and drained
> 10 ounces (one 16-ounce can) red kidney beans, rinsed and drained
> ½ cup chopped onion
> ½ cup chopped green bell pepper
> ½ cup Kraft Fat Free Italian Dressing
> Sugar substitute to equal 1 tablespoon sugar

In a large bowl, combine green beans, wax beans, kidney beans, onion, and green pepper. Add Italian dressing and sugar substitute. Mix well to combine. Cover and refrigerate for at least 30 minutes. Gently stir again just before serving.

Each serving equals:

HE: 1¼ Vegetable • ⅔ Protein • 9 Optional Calories

52 Calories • 0 gm Fat • 2 gm Protein •
11 gm Carbohydrate • 242 mg Sodium • 29 mg Calcium •
3 gm Fiber

DIABETIC: 1 Vegetable • ½ Starch/Carbohydrate

Sauerkraut Salad

Here's a wonderful side dish for any meal that features frankfurters or sausage. The teaspoon of caraway seed is a real Bavarian-style touch, and you'll be delighted at how much extra flavor it adds to this chilled kraut blend. ☻ Serves 4 (full ¾ cup)

> 2 cups (one 16-ounce can) sauerkraut, drained and chopped
> 1 cup chopped celery
> ½ cup chopped onion
> ½ cup chopped green bell pepper
> 1 teaspoon caraway seed
> ½ teaspoon prepared horseradish sauce
> ¼ cup (one 2-ounce jar) chopped pimiento, drained
> Sugar substitute to equal 2 tablespoons sugar

In a medium bowl, combine sauerkraut, celery, onion, and green pepper. Add caraway seed, horseradish sauce, pimiento, and sugar substitute. Mix well to combine. Cover and refrigerate for 24 hours. Gently stir again just before serving.

Each serving equals:

HE: 2 Vegetable

48 Calories • 0 gm Fat • 2 gm Protein •
10 gm Carbohydrate • 808 mg Sodium •
57 mg Calcium • 4 gm Fiber

DIABETIC: 2 Vegetable

Green Pepper Ham Salad Cups

Stuffed peppers are a tradition in most families, but have you ever considered stuffing them with a rich and creamy ham salad? This attractive dish delivers lots of good nutrition for not a lot of calories—and it tastes oh-so-scrumptious! ☻ Serves 4

> 2 medium-sized green bell peppers
> 1 (8-ounce) package Philadelphia fat-free cream cheese
> 1½ cups (9 ounces) finely diced Dubuque 97% fat-free ham or any
>   extra-lean ham
> 1 cup finely chopped celery
> 2 tablespoons chopped fresh parsley or 2 teaspoons dried parsley
>   flakes
> 2 tablespoons Kraft Fat Free French Dressing

Cut the green peppers in half lengthwise and remove the seeds and membrane. In a medium bowl, stir cream cheese with a spoon until soft. Add ham, celery, and parsley. Mix well to combine. Stir in French dressing. Spoon the mixture into the green pepper halves. Cover and refrigerate for at least 30 minutes.

Each serving equals:

HE: 2½ Protein • 1½ Vegetable • 12 Optional Calories

122 Calories • 2 gm Fat • 19 gm Protein •
7 gm Carbohydrate • 808 mg Sodium • 18 mg Calcium •
1 gm Fiber

DIABETIC: 2½ Meat • 2 Vegetable

Sweet Salads

I was raised to celebrate the great Midwestern tradition of serving sweet salads at just about every lunch, dinner, or Sunday supper. If the Ladies' Auxiliary at the church was holding a luncheon, there'd always be an abundance of vividly colorful Jell-O salads decorating the buffet table. And whether company was coming for Thanksgiving turkey or an afternoon card party, a pretty gelatin dish was not only expected but welcomed with pleasure!

There's hardly a church or community cookbook that doesn't feature a number of sweet salads in its pages. Even if you're used to eating these sweet dishes as a dessert rather than an accompaniment, why not give these palate-pleasing recipes a try?

I hope you'll enjoy the dazzling variety of salads in this section, from lovely cottage cheese salads both sweet and tart (like my Snowflake Salad) to fruited concoctions as colorful as they are tasty (Frozen Fruit Salad is a great one to try). They're as refreshing as a cool summer breeze, and they look especially festive on your table.

Sweet Salads

Apple Gelatin Salad

Have you ever wished for a JELL-O flavor the company just hasn't invented? I always wanted an apple-flavored gelatin dish, and so I just had to create one! This lovely salad is full of nutty, fruity crunch and looks extra-special on the plate.　　❂　　Serves 8

3 cups unsweetened apple juice ☆
1 cup water
2 (4-serving) packages JELL-O sugar-free lemon gelatin
1 cup (2 small) cored, unpeeled, and chopped Red Delicious apples
¼ cup (1 ounce) chopped pecans
1 cup chopped celery

In a medium saucepan, bring 2 cups apple juice and water to a boil. Remove from heat. Add dry gelatin. Mix well to dissolve gelatin. Stir in remaining 1 cup apple juice. Add apples, pecans, and celery. Mix well to combine. Pour mixture into an 8-by-8-inch dish. Refrigerate until firm, about 3 hours. Cut into 8 servings.

HINT:　　Good topped with 1 teaspoon fat-free mayonnaise, but don't forget to count the few additional calories.

Each serving equals:

HE: 1 Fruit　•　½ Fat　•　½ Vegetable　•
10 Optional Calories

---

91 Calories　•　3 gm Fat　•　1 gm Protein　•
15 gm Carbohydrate　•　71 mg Sodium　•　17 mg Calcium　•
1 gm Fiber

DIABETIC: 1 Fruit　•　½ Fat　•　½ Vegetable

Carrot-Pineapple Salad

What could be more colorful and fun than this bright square of sun-shine-on-a-plate? You get your healthy fruit and veggies in every fresh bite, and somehow every other dish is brightened by its presence at the meal!   ☻   Serves 6

1 (4-serving) package JELL-O sugar-free orange gelatin
1 cup boiling water
1 cup (one 8-ounce can) crushed pineapple, packed in fruit juice, and
    1/4 cup liquid reserved
1/2 cup cold water
1 1/2 cups shredded carrots

In a medium bowl, combine dry gelatin and boiling water. Mix well to dissolve gelatin. Stir in reserved pineapple liquid and cold water. Add pineapple and carrots. Mix well to combine. Pour mixture into an 8-by-8-inch dish. Refrigerate until firm, about 3 hours. Cut into 6 servings.

Each serving equals:

HE: 1/2 Vegetable • 1/3 Fruit • 7 Optional Calories

44 Calories • 0 gm Fat • 1 gm Protein •
10 gm Carbohydrate • 46 mg Sodium • 13 mg Calcium •
1 gm Fiber

DIABETIC: 1/2 Starch/Carbohydrate

Evergreen Pear Salad

The soft green hue of this extra-creamy lime-flavored salad is downright irresistible! It's light and sweet, a wonderful palate pleaser, and just right for so many summer celebrations. ☻ Serves 6

> 2 cups (one 16-ounce can) pears, packed in fruit juice, drained and
>   chopped, and ¾ cup liquid reserved
> 1 (4-serving) package JELL-O sugar-free lime gelatin
> 1 cup cold water
> ½ cup (4 ounces) Philadelphia fat-free cream cheese, softened
> ¾ cup Cool Whip Free

In a small saucepan, bring reserved pear juice to a boil. Remove from heat. Add dry gelatin. Mix well to dissolve gelatin. Stir in water. Reserve ½ cup gelatin mixture in a large bowl and place in refrigerator. Stir pears into remaining gelatin mixture. Pour mixture into an 8-by-8-inch dish. Refrigerate. When the reserved ½ cup gelatin mixture starts to thicken, stir in cream cheese, using a wire whisk. Add Cool Whip Free. Mix well to combine. Spread mixture over partially set pear-gelatin mixture. Refrigerate until firm, about 2 hours. Cut into 6 servings.

Each serving equals:

HE: ⅔ Fruit • ⅓ Protein • 17 Optional Calories

80 Calories • 0 gm Fat • 4 gm Protein •
16 gm Carbohydrate • 157 mg Sodium • 4 mg Calcium •
2 gm Fiber

DIABETIC: 1 Fruit *or* 1 Starch/Carbohydrate

Cottage Cherry Salad

Here's a pretty, old-style salad that is both sweet and tart with the luscious flavor of cherries! Make sure you let the cherry mixture cool all the way, so you don't curdle the cottage cheese when you blend the two into pink perfection. ☻ Serves 8 (¾ cup)

1 (4-serving) package JELL-O sugar-free vanilla cook-and-serve pudding mix
1 (4-serving) package JELL-O sugar-free cherry gelatin
2 cups (one 16-ounce can) tart red cherries, packed in water, drained, and ½ cup liquid reserved
¾ cup water
1 teaspoon almond extract
2 cups fat-free cottage cheese
1 cup Cool Whip Free

In a medium saucepan, combine dry pudding mix, dry gelatin, reserved cherry liquid, and water. Stir in cherries. Cook over medium heat until mixture thickens and starts to boil, stirring often, and being careful not to crush the cherries. Remove from heat. Stir in almond extract. Place saucepan on a wire rack and allow to cool completely. In a medium bowl, combine cottage cheese and Cool Whip Free. Blend in cooled cherry mixture. Refrigerate for at least 30 minutes. Gently stir again just before serving.

Each serving equals:

HE: ½ Protein • ½ Fruit • ¼ Slider •
10 Optional Calories

88 Calories • 0 gm Fat • 9 gm Protein •
13 gm Carbohydrate • 305 mg Sodium •
31 mg Calcium • 0 gm Fiber

DIABETIC: 1 Meat • ½ Starch/Carbohydrate • ½ Fruit

Fruit Fantasy Salad

This is such a simple way to jazz up a luncheon plate, especially when unexpected guests arrive. There's no waiting time as with a gelatin salad—just spoon out the fruit, stir up the creamy topping, and you've got a real dream of a dish!　　●　　Serves 4

> *Lettuce greens*
> *2 cups (one 16-ounce can) fruit cocktail, packed in fruit juice,*
>   *drained, and 2 tablespoons liquid reserved*
> *¼ cup (1 ounce) chopped walnuts*
> *½ cup (4 ounces) Philadelphia fat-free cream cheese*
> *Sugar substitute to equal 2 teaspoons sugar*

Evenly divide lettuce greens among 4 salad plates. In a medium bowl, combine fruit cocktail and walnuts. Spoon about ⅓ cup of mixture on each plate. In a small bowl, stir cream cheese with a spoon until soft. Add sugar substitute and reserved fruit cocktail liquid. Mix well until smooth. Evenly spoon mixture over fruit mixture. Serve at once.

Each serving equals:

HE: 1 Fruit • ¾ Protein • ½ Fat • 1 Optional Calorie

---

128 Calories • 4 gm Fat • 6 gm Protein •
17 gm Carbohydrate • 176 mg Sodium •
17 mg Calcium • 2 gm Fiber

DIABETIC: 1 Fruit • 1 Fat • ½ Meat

Maple Waldorf Fruit Salad

I have always loved inventing variations on the classic Waldorf salad based on chopped apples, and this one is a new favorite of mine. The dressing is pure New England with its touch of maple and nuts, while the wonderful crunch of apples and celery is just part of the story—the banana and raisins tell the rest!　　●　　Serves 8 (½ cup)

> 2 cups (4 small) unpeeled, cored, and diced Red Delicious apples
> 1 cup (1 medium) diced banana
> ¼ cup raisins
> 1 cup chopped celery
> ½ cup Kraft fat-free mayonnaise
> ¼ cup Cary's Sugar Free Maple Syrup
> ¼ cup Peter Pan reduced-fat peanut butter

In a large bowl, combine apples, banana, raisins, and celery. In a small bowl, combine mayonnaise, maple syrup, and peanut butter. Mix well until smooth. Add mayonnaise mixture to apple mixture. Mix gently to combine. Cover and refrigerate for at least 30 minutes. Gently stir again just before serving.

HINTS: 1. To prevent banana from turning brown, mix with 1 teaspoon lemon juice or sprinkle with Fruit Fresh.

2. To plump up raisins without "cooking," place in a glass measuring cup and microwave on HIGH for 20 seconds.

Each serving equals:

HE: 1 Fruit • ½ Protein • ½ Fat • ¼ Vegetable • 15 Optional Calories

115 Calories • 3 gm Fat • 2 gm Protein • 20 gm Carbohydrate • 198 mg Sodium • 11 mg Calcium • 2 gm Fiber

DIABETIC: 1 Fruit • ½ Starch/Carbohydrate • ½ Fat

Fall Waldorf Salad

Chopped fresh pears at their ripe best are a mouth-pleasing addition to this Waldorf version, which is special enough to be served in the New York hotel that often hosts the president! I think you'll agree that the cinnamon in this tasty combo makes it absolutely delectable!

○ Serves 4 (full ¾ cup)

½ cup Kraft fat-free mayonnaise
¼ cup Cool Whip Free
¼ teaspoon ground cinnamon
1½ cups (3 small) cored and diced Bartlett pears
½ cup (1 small) unpeeled, cored and diced Red Delicious apple
1 cup diced celery
¼ cup (1 ounce) chopped walnuts

In a large bowl, combine mayonnaise, Cool Whip Free, and cinnamon. Add pears, apple, celery, and walnuts. Mix well to combine. Cover and refrigerate for at least 30 minutes. Gently stir again just before serving.

Each serving equals:

HE: 1 Fruit • ½ Fat • ½ Slider • 15 Optional Calories

130 Calories • 4 gm Fat • 1 gm Protein •
23 gm Carbohydrate • 346 mg Sodium •
26 mg Calcium • 3 gm Fiber

DIABETIC: 1 Fruit • 1 Fat • ½ Starch/Carbohydrate

Snowflake Salad

Can you imagine serving this light and pretty salad on a chilly winter day when all you're dreaming of is summer? There's just something about the flavors of lemon and pineapple that brighten up any occasion!   ☻   Serves 6

> 2 cups (two 8-ounce cans) crushed pineapple, packed in fruit juice,
>   drained, and ½ cup liquid reserved ☆
> 1 (4-serving) package JELL-O sugar-free lemon gelatin
> 1½ cups fat-free cottage cheese
> 1 cup Cool Whip Free ☆

In a medium saucepan, combine reserved pineapple liquid and ¾ cup drained pineapple. Bring mixture to a boil. Remove from heat. Add dry gelatin. Mix well to dissolve gelatin. Refrigerate for 30 minutes or until gelatin starts to thicken. Fold cottage cheese and ½ cup Cool Whip Free into partially set gelatin. Pour mixture into an 8-by-8-inch dish. Refrigerate until firm, about 3 hours. In a small bowl, combine remaining ½ cup Cool Whip Free and remaining drained pineapple. Spread topping mixture evenly over set gelatin and refrigerate for an additional 10 minutes. Cut into 6 servings.

Each serving equals:

HE: ⅔ Fruit • ½ Protein • ¼ Slider •
13 Optional Calories

108 Calories • 0 gm Fat • 7 gm Protein •
20 gm Carbohydrate • 219 mg Sodium •
32 mg Calcium • 1 gm Fiber

DIABETIC: 1 Meat • 1 Fruit

Pistachio–Cottage Cheese Salad

This pretty salad is so full of surprises, each spoonful will bring a smile to your guests' lips! It's a great accompaniment when you're serving a pale-colored main dish like fish or chicken.

◑ Serves 8 (½ cup)

> 1 (4-serving) package JELL-O sugar-free instant pistachio pudding mix
> 2 cups fat-free cottage cheese
> 1 cup (one 8-ounce can) crushed pineapple, packed in fruit juice, undrained
> ¼ cup (1 ounce) chopped pecans
> ½ cup (1 ounce) miniature marshmallows
> 1 cup Cool Whip Free

In a large bowl, combine dry pudding mix and cottage cheese. Add undrained pineapple, pecans, and marshmallows. Mix well to combine. Blend in Cool Whip Free. Refrigerate for at least 30 minutes. Gently stir again just before serving.

Each serving equals:

HE: ½ Protein • ½ Fat • ¼ Fruit • ¼ Slider • 14 Optional Calories

124 Calories • 4 gm Fat • 8 gm Protein • 14 gm Carbohydrate • 373 mg Sodium • 30 mg Calcium • 0 gm Fiber

DIABETIC: 1 Meat • 1 Starch/Carbohydrate • ½ Fat

Frozen Fruit Salad

When it's oh-so-steamy outside, here's a perfect summer delight that is easier to prepare now than when Grandma was young—if only because we have the convenience of fresh frozen berries all year round! This chilled fruit concoction is full of color and crunch, just right for a Fourth of July barbecue with friends! ☻ Serves 6

> 1 (8-ounce) package Philadelphia fat-free cream cheese
> Sugar substitute to equal 4 teaspoons sugar
> 2 cups frozen unsweetened strawberries, partially thawed and
>   chopped, undrained
> 1 cup (one 8-ounce can) crushed pineapple, packed in fruit juice,
>   drained
> 1 cup (1 medium) sliced banana
> ¼ cup (1 ounce) chopped pecans
> 1 cup Cool Whip Free

In a large bowl, stir cream cheese with a spoon until soft. Stir in sugar substitute. Add strawberries, pineapple, banana, and pecans. Mix well to combine. Blend in Cool Whip Free. Pour mixture into an 8-by-8-inch dish. Cover and freeze. Remove from freezer about 10 minutes before serving. Cut into 6 servings.

HINT: To prevent banana from turning brown, mix with 1 teaspoon lemon juice or sprinkle with Fruit Fresh.

Each serving equals:

> HE: 1 Fruit • ⅔ Protein • ⅔ Fat • ¼ Slider •
> 1 Optional Calorie
>
> ---
>
> 152 Calories • 4 gm Fat • 6 gm Protein •
> 23 gm Carbohydrate • 234 mg Sodium •
> 16 mg Calcium • 2 gm Fiber
>
> ---
>
> DIABETIC: 1 Fruit • ½ Starch/Carbohydrate • ½ Meat •
> ½ Fat

Festive Macaroni Salad

If you've never tasted a sweet macaroni salad, this one is certain to surprise and please you and your kids! Fruity and creamy, it's a light and sparkling side dish that's great to serve at a birthday party.

◐ Serves 8 (¾ cup)

> 3 cups cold cooked elbow macaroni, rinsed and drained
> ½ cup (1 ounce) miniature marshmallows
> 2 cups (two 8-ounce cans) crushed pineapple, packed in fruit juice, drained, and ½ cup liquid reserved
> 6 maraschino cherries, quartered
> 1 (4-serving) package JELL-O sugar-free vanilla cook-and-serve pudding mix
> 1 cup water
> 1 cup Cool Whip Free

In a large bowl, combine macaroni, marshmallows, pineapple, and cherries. Cover and refrigerate. Meanwhile, in a medium saucepan, combine dry pudding mix, reserved pineapple liquid, and water. Cook over medium heat until mixture thickens and starts to boil, stirring often. Remove from heat. Place pan on a wire rack and allow to cool for 5 minutes. Pour slightly cooled pudding mixture over macaroni mixture. Mix well to combine. Refrigerate for at least 2 hours. Just before serving, stir in Cool Whip Free.

HINT: 2 cups uncooked elbow macaroni usually cooks to about 3 cups.

Each serving equals:

> HE: ¾ Bread • ½ Fruit • ¼ Slider •
> 19 Optional Calories
>
> ---
>
> 156 Calories • 0 gm Fat • 3 gm Protein •
> 36 gm Carbohydrate • 173 mg Sodium •
> 13 mg Calcium • 1 gm Fiber
>
> ---
>
> DIABETIC: 1½ Starch/Carbohydrate • ½ Fruit
> *or* 2 Starch/Carbohydrate

Vegetables

"Eat your vegetables," Mother always used to say, but Grandma understood better than anyone that you'd be happy to gobble them down if they were stirred up in scrumptious sauces and baked to a golden brown in her oven! My Grandma believed in sharing the abundant harvest with her family and her guests, and her table was always laden with home-style dishes that made everyone's mouth water!

What's great about comfort food cooking the Healthy Exchanges way is that you don't need to put in nearly as much time as Grandma did over a hot stove or peeking into the oven to check on a casserole. You don't have to make everything from scratch in order to make it cozy and delicious, but if you're tired of the same old green beans and potatoes, I invite you to look at vegetables the way they used to be!

Whether your taste buds are longing for a cheesy potato casserole served steaming hot from the oven (my Classic Potato Casserole will do the trick!) or could be tempted by a tangy skillet blend like Grandma's Home-Style Green Beans, this section will remind you just how delectable "eating your veggies" can be again!

Vegetables

Old-Fashioned Stewed Tomatoes ❄

I love tomatoes fresh, I love tomatoes cooked, and I especially enjoy them stewed just the way my grandma used to prepare them—a little bit sweet, and in a dish with cubes of bread that soak up all their tasty juices! This is such an easy way to get that old-time flavor, I bet you'll make this dish a regular on your menu. ☻ Serves 4 (¾ cup)

> 3½ cups (two 14½-ounce cans) stewed tomatoes, undrained
> 1 teaspoon dried parsley flakes
> ½ teaspoon black pepper
> 2 teaspoons Sugar Twin or Sprinkle Sweet
> 2 slices stale reduced-calorie white bread, cut into cubes

In a medium saucepan, combine undrained stewed tomatoes, parsley flakes, and black pepper. Bring mixture to a boil. Lower heat. Stir in Sugar Twin. Add bread cubes. Mix well to combine. Continue cooking for 5 minutes or until mixture is heated through, stirring often.

Each serving equals:

HE: 1¾ Vegetable • ¼ Bread • 1 Optional Calorie

80 Calories • 0 gm Fat • 3 gm Protein •
17 gm Carbohydrate • 688 mg Sodium •
122 mg Calcium • 3 gm Fiber

DIABETIC: 1 Vegetable • ½ Starch/Carbohydrate

Company Green Beans
with Mushrooms

Lemon pepper is one of my favorite culinary tricks, and you'll see how well it works in this yummy green bean dish! All these flavors join hands to say "welcome" and to show how much you enjoy sharing dinner with your friends. ☻ Serves 2 (1 full cup)

> 2 tablespoons finely chopped onion
> 2 cups (one 16-ounce can) cut green beans, rinsed and drained
> ¼ cup (one 2-ounce jar) chopped pimiento, drained
> 1 teaspoon dried parsley flakes
> ½ cup (one 2.5-ounce jar) sliced mushrooms, drained
> ⅛ teaspoon lemon pepper

In a medium skillet sprayed with butter-flavored cooking spray, sauté onion for 5 minutes or until tender. Add green beans, pimiento, parsley flakes, mushrooms, and lemon pepper. Mix well to combine. Continue cooking for 5 minutes, or until mixture is heated through, stirring often.

Each serving equals:

HE: 2¾ Vegetable

56 Calories • 0 gm Fat • 3 gm Protein •
11 gm Carbohydrate • 172 mg Sodium •
52 mg Calcium • 4 gm Fiber

DIABETIC: 2 Vegetable

Grandma's Home-Style Green Beans

In earlier times, Grandma might cook up a pot of veggies with a ham hock tossed in for extra-special flavor. These days, we can enjoy that taste of ham without all the extra fat—especially in this hearty dish of beans and potatoes!   ☻   Serves 4 (1½ cups)

> 1 full cup (6 ounces) diced Dubuque 97% fat-free ham or any extra-lean ham
> 5 cups frozen or fresh cut green beans
> 3 cups (15 ounces) diced raw potatoes
> ½ cup finely chopped onion
> 1 cup water
> ¼ teaspoon black pepper
> 2 or 3 drops Tabasco sauce

In a large saucepan sprayed with butter-flavored cooking spray, sauté ham for 5 minutes. Add green beans, potatoes, onion, and water. Mix well to combine. Bring mixture to a boil. Stir in black pepper and Tabasco sauce. Lower heat, cover, and simmer until beans and potatoes are tender and most of liquid is absorbed, stirring occasionally.

Each serving equals:

HE: 2¾ Vegetable • 1 Protein • ¾ Bread

---

145 Calories • 1 gm Fat • 10 gm Protein • 24 gm Carbohydrate • 369 mg Sodium • 56 mg Calcium • 4 gm Fiber

---

DIABETIC: 2 Vegetable • 1 Starch • 1 Meat

Barbecued Green Beans with Canadian Bacon

Cliff came looking to see what was cooking in the kitchen when I was testing this tasty recipe. Maybe it was the irresistible aroma of my homemade barbecue sauce, or that touch of smokiness that Canadian bacon provides. But let me tell you, I didn't have to ring the dinner bell more than once that evening!   ☻   Serves 4

½ cup chopped onion

1 cup (5 ounces) diced lean Canadian bacon

4 cups (two 16-ounce cans) cut green beans, rinsed and drained

1 cup (one 8-ounce can) Hunt's Tomato Sauce

2 tablespoons Brown Sugar Twin

2 tablespoons Sugar Twin or Sprinkle Sweet

1 teaspoon prepared mustard

2 tablespoons white vinegar

¼ teaspoon black pepper

Preheat oven to 350 degrees. Spray an 8-by-8-inch baking dish with butter-flavored cooking spray. In a large skillet sprayed with butter-flavored cooking spray, sauté onion and Canadian bacon for 5 minutes. Stir in green beans. Add tomato sauce, Brown Sugar Twin, Sugar Twin, mustard, vinegar, and black pepper. Mix well to combine. Pour mixture into prepared baking dish. Bake for 45 minutes. Place baking dish on a wire rack and let set for 5 minutes. Divide into 4 servings.

Each serving equals:

HE: 3¼ Vegetable • 1¼ Protein • 5 Optional Calories

111 Calories • 3 gm Fat • 9 gm Protein •
12 gm Carbohydrate • 919 mg Sodium •
44 mg Calcium • 3 gm Fiber

DIABETIC: 2 Vegetable • 1 Meat

Creamy Cookstove Carrots

Here's an old-fashioned dish that is equally good whether you make it with fresh carrots from your garden or farm stand, or with a bag of frozen carrots from the market. Make sure you cook them until they're tender, not too soft, and just listen to the oohs and aahs when you serve this luscious recipe!   ☻   Serves 6 (¾ cup)

1 cup chopped onion

5 cups fresh or frozen cut carrots

2 tablespoons chopped fresh parsley or 2 teaspoons dried parsley flakes

1¾ cups (one 14½-ounce can) Swanson Beef Broth

1 (10¾-ounce) can Healthy Request Cream of Mushroom Soup

In a large skillet sprayed with butter-flavored cooking spray, sauté onion for 5 minutes or until tender. Add carrots, parsley, and beef broth. Mix well to combine. Cover and cook over medium heat for 20 minutes. Uncover. Stir in mushroom soup. Continue cooking for 10 to 12 minutes or until carrots are tender, stirring occasionally.

Each serving equals:

HE: 2 Vegetable • ¼ Slider • 13 Optional Calories

82 Calories • 2 gm Fat • 2 gm Protein •
14 gm Carbohydrate • 493 mg Sodium •
76 mg Calcium • 2 gm Fiber

DIABETIC: 2 Vegetable • 1½ Starch/Carbohydrate

Boarding House
Creamed Peas and Carrots

There's just something so cozy about creamed vegetables, maybe because that rich sauce hugging your peas and carrots was like getting a real hug from Grandma! You'll be delighted to see how thick and rich this dish gets when you blend the evaporated skim milk and the flour. It's another cooking secret worthy of Grandma's kitchen!

○ Serves 6 (full ½ cup)

1½ cups frozen sliced carrots
1½ cups water
1½ cups frozen peas
1½ cups (one 12-fluid-ounce can) Carnation Evaporated Skim Milk
3 tablespoons all-purpose flour
1 teaspoon dried parsley flakes
¼ teaspoon lemon pepper
½ teaspoon Sugar Twin or Sprinkle Sweet

In a medium saucepan, cook carrots in water for 15 minutes. Add peas. Continue cooking for 5 minutes. Drain. In a covered jar, combine evaporated skim milk and flour. Shake well to blend. Pour milk mixture into same saucepan sprayed with butter-flavored cooking spray. Add parsley flakes, lemon pepper, and Sugar Twin. Mix well to combine. Cook for 2 to 3 minutes, stirring constantly. Stir drained peas and carrots into milk mixture. Continue cooking until mixture thickens, stirring often.

Each serving equals:

HE: ⅔ Bread • ½ Vegetable • ½ Skim Milk

100 Calories • 0 gm Fat • 7 gm Protein •
18 gm Carbohydrate • 91 mg Sodium •
205 mg Calcium • 3 gm Fiber

DIABETIC: 1 Starch/Carbohydrate *or*
½ Starch • ½ Vegetable • ½ Skim Milk

Broccoli-Cheese Casserole

Bet you think that this cheesy broccoli dish would probably be "good enough" if I had you melt some reduced-fat cheddar over those good-for-you green veggies. But I like to say that "good enough" isn't good enough for me, so I stir in a little fat-free sour cream to give this quick casserole the taste of truly homemade! ☻ Serves 6

> 1 (10¾-ounce) can Healthy Request Cream of Mushroom Soup
> 1½ cups (6 ounces) shredded Kraft reduced-fat Cheddar cheese
> ⅓ cup skim milk
> 1 teaspoon Worcestershire sauce
> ⅓ cup Land O Lakes no-fat sour cream
> 1 cup (3 ounces) uncooked Minute Rice
> 3 cups frozen cut broccoli, slightly thawed

Preheat oven to 350 degrees. Spray an 8-by-8-inch baking dish with butter-flavored cooking spray. In a large saucepan, combine mushroom soup, Cheddar cheese, skim milk, and Worcestershire sauce. Cook over medium heat until cheese melts, stirring constantly. Remove from heat. Add sour cream and uncooked rice. Mix well to combine. Stir in broccoli. Pour mixture into prepared baking dish. Cover and bake for 30 minutes. Uncover and continue baking for 15 minutes. Place baking dish on a wire rack and let set for 5 minutes. Divide into 6 servings.

Each serving equals:

> HE: 1¼ Protein • 1 Vegetable • ½ Bread • ½ Slider • 6 Optional Calories
> _____
> 162 Calories • 6 gm Fat • 11 gm Protein •
> 16 gm Carbohydrate • 506 mg Sodium •
> 292 mg Calcium • 1 gm Fiber
> _____
> DIABETIC: 1 Meat • 1 Vegetable • 1 Starch/Carbohydrate

Eastern Europe Beets

One of the tastiest traditions the immigrants from Eastern Europe brought with them to America were dishes as tangy and rich as this special way to serve beets! If you like your taste buds tingling, you may want to experiment with a dab more horseradish, but be careful—it packs a real punch!   ☾   Serves 2 (Scant ½ cup)

> 2 tablespoons Land O Lakes no-fat sour cream
> 1 teaspoon prepared horseradish sauce
> ¼ teaspoon dried dill weed
> 1 cup (one 8-ounce can) beets, diced and drained

In a medium bowl, combine sour cream, horseradish sauce, and dill weed. Add beets. Mix gently to combine. Cover and refrigerate for at least 30 minutes. Gently stir again just before serving.

Each serving equals:

HE: 1 Vegetable • 18 Optional Calories

40 Calories • 0 gm Fat • 1 gm Protein •
9 gm Carbohydrate • 254 mg Sodium •
32 mg Calcium • 2 gm Fiber

DIABETIC: 1 Vegetable

Classic Potato Casserole

My grandma often served scalloped potato casseroles like this golden-crusted delight, and it's a family tradition we've kept even though we're eating healthy! Just a spoonful of this dish will persuade your fussiest eaters that old-fashioned flavor is alive and well at your house!

◐ Serves 6

6 cups (20 ounces) shredded loose-packed frozen potatoes, thawed

¾ cup chopped onion

2 teaspoons dried parsley flakes

1½ cups (6 ounces) shredded Kraft reduced-fat Cheddar cheese

1 cup Kraft fat-free mayonnaise

1 (10¾-ounce) can Healthy Request Cream of Mushroom Soup

Preheat oven to 350 degrees. Spray an 8-by-8-inch baking dish with butter-flavored cooking spray. In a very large bowl, combine potatoes, onion, parsley flakes, and Cheddar cheese. Add mayonnaise and mushroom soup. Mix well to combine. Spread mixture into prepared baking dish. Cover and bake for 60 minutes. Uncover and continue baking for 15 minutes. Place baking dish on a wire rack and let set for 5 minutes. Divide into 6 servings.

HINT: Mr. Dell's frozen shredded potatoes are a good choice for this recipe, or raw shredded potatoes may be used in place of frozen.

Each serving equals:

HE: 2 Protein • ⅔ Bread • ¼ Vegetable • ½ Slider • 14 Optional Calories

219 Calories • 7 gm Fat • 10 gm Protein • 29 gm Carbohydrate • 808 mg Sodium • 243 mg Calcium • 2 gm Fiber

DIABETIC: 2 Starch/Carbohydrate • 1 Meat

Hawaiian Sweet Potatoes

Sweet potatoes are one of Mother Nature's best efforts, because they're so naturally sweet before you stir in anything at all! But because too much of a good thing can be wonderful, why not sweeten them up even more with this taste treat inspired by memories of Maui! You'll be so glad you did! ☻ Serves 4 (¾ cup)

> 2 cups (12 ounces) diced cooked sweet potatoes
> 1 cup (one 8-ounce can) crushed pineapple, packed in fruit juice,
>   drained, and ¼ cup liquid reserved
> 2 tablespoons Brown Sugar Twin
> 2 tablespoons flaked coconut

In an 8-cup glass microwavable measuring bowl, combine sweet potatoes, pineapple, and reserved pineapple juice. Sprinkle Brown Sugar Twin and coconut evenly over top. Cover and microwave on HIGH (100 percent power) for 4 to 5 minutes or until heated through, turning bowl after 2 minutes. Uncover and let set 2 to 3 minutes.

Each serving equals:

HE: ⅔ Bread • ⅓ Fruit • 10 Optional Calories

125 Calories • 1 gm Fat • 2 gm Protein •
27 gm Carbohydrate • 52 mg Sodium • 28 mg Calcium •
3 gm Fiber

DIABETIC: 1½ Starch/Carbohydrate

Main Dishes

Take a minute to remember with me that wonderful moment when you turned toward the kitchen door and waited for Grandma to set a steaming platter in the center of the table. The delicious aromas emerging from her kitchen had already provided a delectable preview of the meal, but when the dish finally arrived, you could almost hear a collective "Mmmm-mmm!" And then, when she began serving her special recipe to each member of the family, there was a touching moment of give and take that I bet you still recall with warm affection.

The dishes our mothers and grandmothers served tasted extra-delicious because they were prepared with loving care. Those meals of comfort foods fed our spirits as much as they did our tummies. But how often does your family sit down to dinner together anymore, and when they do, how long do they stay at the table before running off to watch television or play video games?

The heart of this book is this section of old-fashioned cozy recipes that taste of home and hearth. When you tempt your family with dishes like Chicken Pie with Stuffing Crust and Bountiful Harvest Stew, you'll be delighted to see that your kids and husband will linger over each tasty bite. The flavors that Grandma welcomed us with are all in here, but prepared in quick and easy ways that everyone can serve with pride!

Main Dishes

Cheesy Macaroni and Tomatoes ❄

Because so many people love adding tomatoes to their grilled-cheese sandwiches, I thought I'd try mixing those gorgeously red veggie-fruits into a slightly untraditional macaroni and cheese! Somehow, their sweet-and-tangy goodness makes a splendid meal even more spectacular! ☻ Serves 4

> ½ cup chopped onion
>
> 2 cups (one 16-ounce can) tomatoes, coarsely chopped and undrained
>
> 1½ cups (one 12-fluid-ounce can) Carnation Evaporated Skim Milk
>
> 3 tablespoons all-purpose flour
>
> ¾ cup (3 ounces) shredded Kraft reduced-fat Cheddar cheese
>
> 2½ cups hot cooked elbow macaroni, rinsed and drained
>
> ⅛ teaspoon black pepper
>
> 1 teaspoon dried parsley flakes

Preheat oven to 350 degrees. Spray an 8-by-8-inch baking dish with butter-flavored cooking spray. In a large skillet sprayed with butter-flavored cooking spray, sauté onion for 5 minutes or until tender. Stir in undrained tomatoes. In a covered jar, combine evaporated skim milk and flour. Shake well to blend. Pour milk mixture into skillet with tomato mixture. Stir in Cheddar cheese. Continue cooking until sauce thickens and cheese melts. Add macaroni, black pepper, and parsley flakes. Mix well to combine. Pour mixture into prepared baking dish. Bake for 20 minutes. Place baking dish on a wire rack and let set for 5 minutes. Divide into 4 servings.

HINT: 1⅔ cups uncooked elbow macaroni usually cooks to about 2½ cups.

Each serving equals:

HE: 1½ Bread • 1¼ Vegetable • ¾ Skim Milk

---

309 Calories • 5 gm Fat • 19 gm Protein •
47 gm Carbohydrate • 315 mg Sodium • 448 mg Calcium •
3 gm Fiber

DIABETIC: 2 Starch • 1 Vegetable • 1 Meat • ½ Skim Milk

Baked Vegetable Hash

If one of your goals is serving meatless entrees more often, here's a perfect dish to test the theory that your family won't even miss the meat! This hearty vegetable combo is so cheesy-rich and golden crusted, it'll seem more like a special treat than a healthful alternative.

● Serves 4

> 1¾ cups water
> ⅓ cup Carnation Nonfat Dry Milk Powder
> 1⅓ cups (3 ounces) instant potato flakes
> 2 cups (one 16-ounce can) sliced carrots, rinsed and drained
> 2 cups (one 16-ounce can) cut green beans, rinsed and drained
> ¾ cup (3 ounces) shredded Kraft reduced-fat Cheddar cheese
> ⅛ teaspoon black pepper

Preheat oven to 350 degrees. Spray an 8-by-8-inch baking dish with butter-flavored cooking spray. In a large saucepan, bring water to a boil. Remove from heat. Add dry milk powder and potato flakes. Mix lightly using a fork. Add carrots, green beans, Cheddar cheese, and black pepper. Mix well to combine. Spread mixture into prepared baking dish. Lightly spray top with butter-flavored cooking spray. Bake for 15 to 20 minutes. Place baking dish on a wire rack and let set for 2 to 3 minutes. Divide into 4 servings.

Each serving equals:

HE: 2 Vegetable • 1 Protein • 1 Bread • ¼ Skim Milk

164 Calories • 4 gm Fat • 10 gm Protein •
22 gm Carbohydrate • 267 mg Sodium •
254 mg Calcium • 3 gm Fiber

DIABETIC: 2 Vegetable • 1 Starch • 1 Meat

Grande Bean Noodle Bake ❄

When you're really, really hungry for a soul-satisfying, truly substantial meal, this spicy casserole will win your heart, and your tummy, too! Beans and cheese, noodles and corn—you'll be well nourished and ready to tackle your toughest chores! ☻ Serves 4

10 ounces (one 16-ounce can) pinto beans, rinsed and drained

½ cup frozen corn

½ cup chunky salsa (mild, medium, or hot)

1 cup (one 8-ounce can) Hunt's Tomato Sauce

2 teaspoons chili seasoning

⅛ teaspoon black pepper

1½ cups hot cooked noodles, rinsed and drained

¾ cup (3 ounces) shredded Kraft reduced-fat Cheddar cheese

Preheat oven to 350 degrees. Spray an 8-by-8-inch baking dish with olive oil–flavored cooking spray. In a large skillet sprayed with olive oil–flavored cooking spray, combine pinto beans, corn, salsa, tomato sauce, chili seasoning, and black pepper. Cook over medium heat for 10 minutes, stirring occasionally. Add noodles. Mix well to combine. Pour mixture into prepared baking dish. Sprinkle Cheddar cheese evenly over top. Bake for 20 to 25 minutes. Place baking dish on a wire rack and let set for 5 minutes. Divide into 4 servings.

HINT: 1¼ cups uncooked noodles usually cooks to about 1½ cups.

Each serving equals:

HE: 2¼ Protein • 1¼ Vegetable • 1 Bread

277 Calories • 5 gm Fat • 16 gm Protein • 42 gm Carbohydrate • 657 mg Sodium • 215 mg Calcium • 8 gm Fiber

DIABETIC: 2 Starch • 1½ Meat • 1 Vegetable

Zucchini Marinara Spaghetti ❄

This is a great way to get all those healthy veggies the Food Pyramid tells us to consume! It's also a great end-of-summer meal that's as thrifty as it is tasty. When the zucchini in your garden is threatening to take over the house, invite lots of friends over and stir up a big pot of this. ☻ Serves 4

½ cup chopped onion
1¾ cups (one 15-ounce can) Hunt's Chunky Tomato Sauce
½ cup water
½ teaspoon dried minced garlic
2 teaspoons Italian seasoning
2 cups diced unpeeled zucchini
2 cups hot cooked spaghetti, rinsed and drained
¼ cup (¾ ounce) grated Kraft fat-free Parmesan cheese

In a large skillet sprayed with olive oil–flavored cooking spray, sauté onion for 5 minutes or until tender. Add tomato sauce, water, garlic, Italian seasoning, and zucchini. Mix well to combine. Lower heat and simmer for 5 minutes or until zucchini is tender, stirring occasionally. For each serving, place ½ cup spaghetti on a plate, spoon about ¾ cup sauce over spaghetti, and sprinkle 1 tablespoon Parmesan cheese over top.

HINT: 1½ cups broken uncooked spaghetti usually cooks to about 2 cups.

Each serving equals:

HE: 3 Vegetable • 1 Bread • ¼ Protein

165 Calories • 1 gm Fat • 6 gm Protein •
33 gm Carbohydrate • 816 mg Sodium •
19 mg Calcium • 5 gm Fiber

DIABETIC: 2 Vegetable • 1½ Starch/Carbohydrate

Italian Baked Fish

Fish this moist and flavorful might seem like a miracle, until you begin with an easy instant marinade, then "shake up" a crust that keeps all that flavor from vanishing during cooking! This works great with any white fish—sole, flounder, cod, halibut—you decide!

● Serves 4

> 6 tablespoons (1½ ounces) dried fine bread crumbs
> 2 teaspoons Italian seasoning
> ¼ cup Kraft Fat Free Italian Dressing
> 16 ounces white fish, cut into 4 pieces
> 1 cup (one 8-ounce can) Hunt's Tomato Sauce

Preheat oven to 350 degrees. Spray an 8-by-8-inch baking dish with butter-flavored cooking spray. In a sealed sandwich bag, combine bread crumbs and Italian seasoning. Pour Italian dressing into a dipping dish. Coat fish pieces in dressing, then place in sandwich bag, one piece at a time, and shake well to coat. Place coated fish pieces in prepared baking dish. Stir any remaining bread crumbs or Italian dressing into tomato sauce. Evenly spoon sauce mixture over top. Bake for 20 to 25 minutes or until fish flakes easily. When serving, evenly spoon sauce over fish.

Each serving equals:

> HE: 1½ Protein • 1 Vegetable • ½ Bread
>
> ---
>
> 170 Calories • 2 gm Fat • 23 gm Protein •
> 15 gm Carbohydrate • 577 mg Sodium •
> 64 mg Calcium • 0 gm Fiber
>
> ---
>
> DIABETIC: 3 Meat • ½ Vegetable • ½ Starch/Carbohydrate

Budget "Lobster"

Here's some more "white fish magic," this time producing a meal that tastes so much like lobster, your family will be astonished! If you've got "caviar" tastes on a "tuna fish" budget, give this unusual dish a try.

◑   Serves 4

> *16 ounces white fish, cut into 4 pieces*
> *2 cups hot water*
> *1 teaspoon salt*
> *2 tablespoons white vinegar*

Place fish pieces in a large saucepan and cover with water. Add salt and vinegar. Mix well to combine. Bring mixture to a boil. Lower heat and simmer for 20 minutes. Carefully remove fish from saucepan and place on broiler of oven. Broil 5 to 6 minutes on each side to dry fish. Lightly spray with butter-flavored cooking spray. Serve at once.

HINTS: 1. Frozen haddock works great.

2. Serve with lemon juice or hot melted reduced-calorie margarine. If using margarine, count accordingly.

Each serving equals:

HE: 1½ Protein

93 Calories • 1 gm Fat • 21 gm Protein •
0 gm Carbohydrate • 625 mg Sodium • 44 mg Calcium •
0 gm Fiber

DIABETIC: 3 Meat

Favorite Tuna Casserole

This classic dish can be prepared in dozens of different ways, but no matter how you stir it up, it stills delivers the flavor that takes you back to childhood memories! The cracker topping is a tradition in my family—how about yours? ☻ Serves 4

> 1 (6-ounce) can white tuna, packed in water, drained and flaked
> 1 cup finely chopped celery
> 1 (10¾-ounce) can Healthy Request Cream of Mushroom Soup
> ¼ cup skim milk
> 1½ cups hot cooked noodles, rinsed and drained
> ¼ teaspoon black pepper
> 5 Ritz Reduced Fat Crackers, made into fine crumbs

Preheat oven to 350 degrees. Spray an 8-by-8-inch baking dish with butter-flavored cooking spray. In a large bowl, combine tuna and celery. Add mushroom soup, skim milk, noodles, and black pepper. Mix well to combine. Pour mixture into prepared baking dish. Evenly sprinkle cracker crumbs over top. Bake for 35 to 40 minutes. Place baking dish on a wire rack and let set for 5 minutes. Divide into 4 servings.

HINT: 1¼ cups uncooked noodles usually cooks to about 1½ cups.

Each serving equals:

> HE: 1 Bread • ¾ Protein • ½ Vegetable • ½ Slider • 7 Optional Calories
>
> ---
> 200 Calories • 4 gm Fat • 15 gm Protein • 26 gm Carbohydrate • 518 mg Sodium • 103 mg Calcium • 1 gm Fiber
>
> ---
> DIABETIC: 1½ Meat • 1½ Starch • ½ Vegetable

Creamy Tuna and Rice

This fast skillet supper is a wonderful choice for supper when everyone's late but still hungry for old-fashioned taste! And you can't beat it when the food budget is stretched, because serving four from one can of tuna is a smart cook's solution.   ❂   Serves 4 (1 full cup)

1 (10¾-ounce) can Healthy Request Cream of Chicken Soup

1 cup skim milk

2 teaspoons reduced-sodium soy sauce

1 (6-ounce) can white tuna, packed in water, drained and flaked

½ cup frozen peas, thawed

¼ cup (one 2-ounce jar) chopped pimiento, drained

¼ teaspoon black pepper

1 cup (3 ounces) uncooked Minute Rice

In a large skillet, combine chicken soup, skim milk, and soy sauce. Stir in tuna, peas, pimiento, and black pepper. Bring mixture to a boil. Remove from heat. Stir in uncooked rice. Cover and let set for 5 minutes. Fluff with a fork before serving.

HINT: Thaw peas by placing in a colander and rinsing under hot water for one minute.

Each serving equals:

HE: 1 Bread • ¾ Protein • ¼ Skim Milk • ½ Slider • 1 Optional Calorie

170 Calories • 2 gm Fat • 16 gm Protein • 22 gm Carbohydrate • 562 mg Sodium • 139 mg Calcium • 1 gm Fiber

DIABETIC: 1½ Starch/Carbohydrate • 1½ Meat

Heritage Salmon Loaf

This is such a wonderful old-timey dish, it just seems to make everyone eating it feel closer to the family members seated around the table! Salmon is such a rich fish, it satisfies the taste buds as perfectly as this crusty and fragrant loaf feeds the eye. ◐ Serves 6

⅔ cup Carnation Nonfat Dry Milk Powder

¾ cup water

1 (14¾-ounce) can pink salmon, drained and flaked

¾ cup finely chopped celery

¼ cup chopped onion

28 small fat-free saltine crackers, made into fine crumbs

1 (10¾-ounce) can Healthy Request Cream of Celery Soup

1 teaspoon dried parsley flakes

Preheat oven to 350 degrees. Spray a 9-by-5-inch loaf pan with butter-flavored cooking spray. In a large bowl, combine dry milk powder and water. Add salmon, celery, onion, crackers, celery soup, and parsley flakes. Mix well to combine. Let set for 2 to 3 minutes for crackers to absorb moisture. Pat mixture into prepared loaf pan. Bake for 40 to 45 minutes. Place loaf pan on a wire rack and let set 5 minutes. Cut into 6 servings.

Each serving equals:

HE: 2⅓ Protein • ⅔ Bread • ⅓ Skim Milk • ⅓ Vegetable • ¼ Slider • 10 Optional Calories

179 Calories • 3 gm Fat • 18 gm Protein • 20 gm Carbohydrate • 766 mg Sodium • 196 mg Calcium • 0 gm Fiber

DIABETIC: 2 Meat • 1½ Starch

Salmon and Broccoli Casserole ❄

This unusual combination of flavors provides great nutrition in a tasty casserole your family will welcome with shining eyes and hungry tummies! Plain stewed tomatoes work great in this recipe, but if you're feeling adventurous, you might stir in a can of the Italian or Cajun variety.   ☺   Serves 6

⅔ cup Carnation Nonfat Dry Milk Powder
1 cup water
3 tablespoons all-purpose flour
½ teaspoon lemon pepper
1 cup (one 8-ounce can) stewed tomatoes, coarsely chopped and
   undrained
3 cups cooked cut broccoli
1 (14¾-ounce) can pink salmon, drained, boned, and flaked
6 tablespoons (1½ ounces) dried fine bread crumbs
1 tablespoon reduced-calorie margarine

Preheat oven to 375 degrees. Spray an 8-by-8-inch baking dish with butter-flavored cooking spray. In a covered jar, combine dry milk powder, water, and flour. Shake well to blend. Pour milk mixture into a saucepan sprayed with butter-flavored cooking spray. Bring mixture to a boil. Stir in lemon pepper and undrained stewed tomatoes. Lower heat and simmer for 5 minutes. Spread broccoli in prepared baking dish. Sprinkle salmon evenly over broccoli. Spoon hot tomato mixture on top. Sprinkle top with bread crumbs and dot with margarine. Bake for 45 minutes. Place casserole on a wire rack and let set for 5 minutes. Divide into 6 servings.

Each serving equals:

HE: 2⅓ Protein • 1⅓ Vegetable • ½ Bread •
⅓ Skim Milk • ¼ Fat

187 Calories • 3 gm Fat • 20 gm Protein •
20 gm Carbohydrate • 850 mg Sodium •
298 mg Calcium • 3 gm Fiber

DIABETIC: 2½ Meat • 1 Vegetable • 1 Starch/Carbohydrate

Cheesy Chicken Casserole

This is so cheesy and creamy, it'll bubble its way into your heart as it bakes! Grandma always served leftover chicken in imaginative ways, so no one ever felt as if leftovers were a "letdown"! And if you decide to let your deli do your "roasting" for you, your family will never suspect.

○ Serves 4

1 cup (3 ounces) uncooked rotini pasta
2 cups frozen carrot, broccoli, and cauliflower blend
3 cups water
1 full cup (6 ounces) diced cooked chicken breast
1 (10¾-ounce) can Healthy Request Cream of Mushroom Soup
¾ cup (3 ounces) shredded Kraft reduced-fat Cheddar cheese
⅛ teaspoon black pepper
½ teaspoon dried parsley flakes

Preheat oven to 350 degrees. Spray an 8-by-8-inch baking dish with butter-flavored cooking spray. In a medium saucepan, cook rotini pasta and vegetables in water for 15 minutes or until tender. Drain. Return mixture to saucepan. Add chicken. Mix well to combine. Stir in mushroom soup, Cheddar cheese, black pepper, and parsley flakes. Pour mixture into prepared baking dish. Bake for 20 minutes. Place baking dish on a wire rack and let set for 5 minutes. Divide into 4 servings.

HINTS: 1. 1 cup frozen cauliflower, ½ cup frozen broccoli, and ½ cup frozen carrots may be used in place of frozen blended vegetables.
2. If you don't have leftovers, purchase a chunk of cooked chicken breast from your local deli.

Each serving equals:

HE: 2½ Protein • 1 Bread • 1 Vegetable • ½ Slider • 1 Optional Calorie

239 Calories • 7 gm Fat • 23 gm Protein • 21 gm Carbohydrate • 550 mg Sodium • 237 mg Calcium • 2 gm Fiber

DIABETIC: 2½ Meat • 1½ Starch • 1 Vegetable

Olden Times Chicken Casserole ❄

Here's a little poem that says it all: nothing else is quite as nice as a casserole of chicken and rice! On a cool fall evening, what hits the spot better than a cozy-warm chicken dish that brings back thoughts of happy days?　　◐　　Serves 4

2 cups (one 16-ounce can) Healthy Request Chicken Broth

⅓ cup Carnation Nonfat Dry Milk Powder

¼ cup water

½ cup finely chopped onion

1 full cup (6 ounces) diced cooked chicken breast

¾ cup (3 ounces) shredded Kraft reduced-fat Cheddar cheese

1 cup (3 ounces) uncooked Minute Rice

¼ teaspoon black pepper

1 teaspoon dried parsley flakes

Preheat oven to 375 degrees. Spray an 8-by-8-inch baking dish with butter-flavored cooking spray. In a large bowl, combine chicken broth, dry milk powder, and water. Stir in onion, and chicken. Add Cheddar cheese, uncooked rice, black pepper, and parsley flakes. Mix well to combine. Pour mixture into prepared baking dish. Cover and bake for 45 minutes. Uncover and continue baking for 15 minutes. Place baking dish on a wire rack and let set for 5 minutes. Divide into 4 servings.

HINT:　　If you don't have leftovers, purchase a chunk of cooked chicken breast from your local deli.

Each serving equals:

HE: 2½ Protein • ¾ Bread • ¼ Skim Milk • ¼ Vegetable • 8 Optional Calories

195 Calories • 7 gm Fat • 25 gm Protein • 10 gm Carbohydrate • 533 mg Sodium • 284 mg Calcium • 1 gm Fiber

DIABETIC: 2½ Meat • 1½ Starch

Chicken Pie with Stuffing Crust ❄

Instead of putting your stuffing inside your chicken, why not put your chicken inside your stuffing? That's the culinary brainstorm that gave birth to this luscious chicken pie! It looks so absolutely gorgeous when you carry it to the table, your kids might wonder if it's somebody's birthday! ☻ Serves 6

> 2 cups (one 16-ounce can) Healthy Request Chicken Broth
> 3 cups (4½ ounces) unseasoned dry bread cubes
> 1 full cup (6 ounces) diced cooked chicken breast
> ¾ cup finely chopped celery
> ⅓ cup (1½ ounces) shredded Kraft reduced-fat Cheddar cheese
> ⅔ cup Carnation Nonfat Dry Milk Powder
> 1 cup water
> 1 egg or equivalent in egg substitute
> 1 teaspoon dried onion flakes
> ⅛ teaspoon black pepper
> ½ teaspoon poultry seasoning
> Dash paprika

Preheat oven to 350 degrees. Spray a 9-inch pie plate with butter-flavored cooking spray. In a medium saucepan, bring chicken broth to a boil. Add bread cubes. Remove from heat and mix well until bread cubes are soft. Cool slightly. Press mixture into prepared pie plate. Bake for 15 minutes or until crust is slightly brown. Place pie plate on a wire rack and let set for 5 minutes. Evenly place chicken in bottom of shell. Sprinkle celery and Cheddar cheese over top. In a medium bowl, combine dry milk powder and water. Add egg, onion flakes, black pepper, and poultry seasoning. Mix well using a wire whisk. Pour milk mixture evenly over top. Sprinkle top with paprika. Bake for 35 to 40 minutes or until golden and a knife inserted in center comes out clean. Place pie plate on a wire rack and let set for 5 minutes. Cut into 6 servings.

HINTS: 1. Pepperidge Farm bread cubes work great.

2. If you don't have leftovers, purchase a chunk of cooked chicken breast.

Each serving equals:

HE: 1½ Protein • 1 Bread • ⅓ Skim Milk • ¼ Vegetable • 11 Optional Calories

192 Calories • 4 gm Fat • 18 gm Protein • 21 gm Carbohydrate • 523 mg Sodium • 153 mg Calcium • 1 gm Fiber

DIABETIC: 1½ Meat • 1½ Starch

Scalloped Chicken and Noodles ❄

This chicken pot pie casserole is so full of creamy goodness, it's hard to believe each serving contains only four grams of fat! Not only that, but you get a nice boost of calcium to build strong bones when you gobble this dish down.   ☺   Serves 4

> 1 (10¾-ounce) can Healthy Request Cream of Chicken Soup
> ⅓ cup Carnation Nonfat Dry Milk Powder
> 1 cup water
> ½ cup finely chopped onion
> 1½ cups hot cooked noodles, rinsed and drained
> ½ cup frozen peas, thawed
> 1 full cup (6 ounces) diced cooked chicken breast
> ½ cup (one 2.5-ounce jar) sliced mushrooms, drained
> 1 teaspoon dried parsley flakes
> ¼ teaspoon black pepper
> 5 Ritz Reduced Fat Crackers, made into crumbs
> ¼ cup (¾ ounce) grated Kraft fat-free Parmesan cheese

Preheat oven to 350 degrees. Spray an 8-by-8-inch baking dish with butter-flavored cooking spray. In a medium saucepan, combine chicken soup, dry milk powder, water, and onion. Cook over medium heat until mixture is heated through, stirring often. Stir in noodles, peas, chicken, mushrooms, parsley flakes, and black pepper. Spread mixture into prepared baking dish. In a small bowl, combine cracker crumbs and Parmesan cheese. Evenly sprinkle cracker mixture over top. Bake for 30 minutes. Place baking dish on a wire rack and let set for 2 to 3 minutes. Divide into 4 servings.

HINTS: 1. 1¼ cups uncooked noodles usually cooks to about 1½ cups.

2. Thaw peas by placing in a colander and rinsing under hot water for one minute.

3. If you don't have leftovers, purchase a chunk of cooked chicken breast from your local deli.

Each serving equals:

HE: 1¾ Protein • 1¼ Bread • ½ Vegetable • ¼ Skim Milk • ½ Slider • 5 Optional Calories

268 Calories • 4 gm Fat • 22 gm Protein • 36 gm Carbohydrate • 565 mg Sodium • 99 mg Calcium • 3 gm Fiber

DIABETIC: 2 Meat • 2 Starch

Turkey Macaroni Calico Skillet ❄

Whether you're feeding a large family or a group of boarders as my grandma used to do, you want to fill their tummies and also make their mouths merry! Here's a perfect holiday leftover idea to use up Thanksgiving turkey in a tasty way. ☻ Serves 6 (1 cup)

> 2 cups (one 16-ounce can) Healthy Request Chicken Broth
>
> 3 tablespoons all-purpose flour
>
> 2/3 cup Carnation Nonfat Dry Milk Powder
>
> 1 cup (one 8-ounce can) sliced carrots, rinsed and drained
>
> 1 teaspoon dried onion flakes
>
> 2 teaspoons dried parsley flakes
>
> 1/8 teaspoon black pepper
>
> 3 cups hot cooked elbow macaroni, rinsed and drained
>
> 1/2 cup frozen peas, thawed
>
> 2 full cups (12 ounces) diced cooked turkey breast

In a covered jar, combine chicken broth, flour, and dry milk powder. Shake well to blend. Pour mixture into a large skillet sprayed with butter-flavored cooking spray. Add carrots, onion flakes, parsley flakes, and black pepper. Mix well to combine. Cook over medium heat until mixture thickens, stirring often. Stir in macaroni, peas, and turkey. Lower heat and simmer for 10 minutes or until mixture is heated through, stirring often.

HINTS: 1. 2 cups uncooked elbow macaroni usually cooks to about 3 cups.

2. Thaw peas by placing in a colander and rinsing under hot water for one minute.

3. If you don't have leftovers, purchase a chunk of cooked turkey breast from your local deli.

Each serving equals:

HE: 2 Protein • 1⅓ Bread • ⅓ Skim Milk •
⅓ Vegetable • 6 Optional Calories

---

251 Calories • 3 gm Fat • 26 gm Protein •
30 gm Carbohydrate • 245 mg Sodium •
116 mg Calcium • 2 gm Fiber

DIABETIC: 2 Meat • 2 Starch

Loose Meat Sandwiches

I've always loved sharing our Iowa food traditions with the rest of the country, and no cookbook inspired by Grandma would be complete without this meaty classic! If you're tired of serving plain old burgers, crumble your ground meat with some broth and onion, and it's a brand-new day! ☻ Serves 6

16 ounces ground 90% lean turkey or beef
1 cup chopped onion
2 cups (one 16-ounce can) Healthy Request Chicken Broth
6 reduced-calorie hamburger buns

In a large skillet sprayed with butter-flavored cooking spray, lightly brown meat. Add onion and chicken broth. Mix well to combine. Lower heat and simmer for 20 minutes or until almost all the broth has evaporated, stirring occasionally. For each sandwich, spoon about ⅓ cup meat mixture on each bun.

Each serving equals:

HE: 2 Protein • 1 Bread • ⅓ Vegetable •
5 Optional Calories

195 Calories • 7 gm Fat • 16 gm Protein •
17 gm Carbohydrate • 392 mg Sodium •
7 mg Calcium • 1 gm Fiber

DIABETIC: 2 Meat • 1 Starch

Timeless Meat Loaf

Whenever meat loaf appears on the menu at JO's Kitchen Cafe, it's requested by nearly every guest—so we know we'd better have plenty prepared! This version is traditional in the best sense of the word. It's the kind of recipe handed down from grandmother to granddaughter in homes all over America. ☻ Serves 6

> *1 cup (one 8-ounce can) Hunt's Tomato Sauce*
> *2 teaspoons white vinegar*
> *2 tablespoons Sugar Twin or Sprinkle Sweet*
> *16 ounces ground 90% lean turkey or beef*
> *¾ cup (3 ounces) dried fine bread crumbs*
> *½ teaspoon black pepper*
> *2 tablespoons dried onion flakes*
> *1 tablespoon Hormel Bacon Bits*
> *1 teaspoon dried parsley flakes*

Preheat oven to 350 degrees. Spray a 9-by-5-inch loaf pan with butter-flavored cooking spray. In a large bowl, combine ⅓ cup tomato sauce, vinegar, and Sugar Twin. Add meat, bread crumbs, black pepper, and onion flakes. Mix well to combine. Pat mixture into prepared loaf pan. Stir bacon bits and parsley flakes into remaining ⅔ cup tomato sauce. Evenly spread sauce mixture over meat loaf. Bake for 45 to 50 minutes. Place loaf pan on a wire rack and let set for 5 minutes. Cut into 6 servings.

Each serving equals:

HE: 2 Protein • ⅔ Vegetable • ⅔ Bread •
11 Optional Calories

175 Calories • 7 gm Fat • 16 gm Protein •
12 gm Carbohydrate • 487 mg Sodium •
32 mg Calcium • 1 gm Fiber

DIABETIC: 2 Meat • ½ Starch • ½ Vegetable

Vegetable Soup Casserole ❄

Cream of mushroom soup should probably carry another line on the label that says "Cooking magic in one little can!" It does make a terrific starting point for many creamy casseroles, and this is no exception. Here, it's stirred into a varied blend of veggies, potatoes, and meat, and the finished dish tastes beautifully homemade. ○ Serves 4

8 ounces ground 90% lean turkey or beef
½ cup diced onion
2 cups finely chopped cabbage
½ cup (one 2.5-ounce jar) sliced mushrooms, drained
1 cup grated carrots
3 cups (10 ounces) shredded loose-packed frozen potatoes
1 (10¾-ounce) can Healthy Request Cream of Mushroom Soup
¼ cup skim milk
2 teaspoons dried parsley flakes
⅓ cup (1½ ounces) shredded Kraft reduced-fat Cheddar cheese

Preheat oven to 350 degrees. Spray an 8-by-8-inch baking dish with butter-flavored cooking spray. In a large skillet sprayed with butter-flavored cooking spray, brown meat. Spoon browned meat into prepared baking dish. Layer onion, cabbage, mushrooms, carrots, and potatoes over top. In a small bowl, combine mushroom soup, skim milk, and parsley flakes. Spoon soup mixture evenly over vegetables. Cover and bake for 60 minutes or until vegetables are almost tender. Uncover, sprinkle Cheddar cheese evenly over top, and continue baking for an additional 15 minutes. Place baking dish on a wire rack and let set for 5 minutes. Divide into 4 servings.

Each serving equals:

HE: 2¼ Vegetable • 2 Protein • ½ Bread • ½ Slider • 7 Optional Calories

240 Calories • 8 gm Fat • 16 gm Protein • 26 gm Carbohydrate • 544 mg Sodium • 169 mg Calcium • 4 gm Fiber

DIABETIC: 2 Vegetable • 2 Meat • 1 Starch

Grandma's Surprise

"What's for dinner, Grandma?" a child's voice asks hopefully, and when Grandma replies "It's a surprise," the child can't help but smile and think of the possibilities! This recipe celebrates good old Midwestern ingenuity, combining a bundle of veggies, some cozy noodles, and a topping of golden cheese into a simple delight. ❤ Serves 6

> 8 ounces ground 90% lean turkey or beef
> ½ cup chopped green bell pepper
> ½ cup chopped onion
> 1¾ cups (one 15-ounce can) Hunt's Chunky Tomato Sauce
> ½ cup (one 2.5-ounce jar) sliced mushrooms, drained
> 1 teaspoon Italian seasoning
> 1 cup frozen whole-kernel corn, thawed
> 2 cups hot cooked noodles, rinsed and drained
> ⅓ cup (1½ ounces) sliced ripe olives
> ¼ teaspoon black pepper
> 6 (¾-ounce) slices Kraft reduced-fat American cheese

Preheat oven to 350 degrees. Spray a 9-by-13-inch baking pan with butter-flavored cooking spray. In a large skillet sprayed with butter-flavored cooking spray, brown meat, green pepper, and onion. Stir in tomato sauce, mushrooms, Italian seasoning, corn, noodles, olives, and black pepper. Spread mixture into prepared baking pan. Evenly place cheese slices over top. Bake for 25 to 30 minutes. Place baking pan on a wire rack and let set for 5 minutes. Divide into 6 servings.

HINTS: 1. Thaw corn by placing in a colander and rinsing under hot water for one minute.

2. 1¾ cups uncooked noodles usually cooks to about 2 cups.

Each serving equals:

HE: 2 Protein • 1⅔ Vegetable • 1 Bread • ¼ Fat

231 Calories • 7 gm Fat • 15 gm Protein •
27 gm Carbohydrate • 962 mg Sodium •
140 mg Calcium • 3 gm Fiber

DIABETIC: 1½ Meat • 1½ Vegetable • 1 Starch • ½ Fat

Top-of-the-Stove Creamy "Pot Roast"

The flavor of old-timey pot roast is unmistakable, but not every cook has time to prepare this family favorite the traditional way. Why not please your family's taste buds tonight with this stove-top dish that recalls the real thing? It's fast, it's flavorful, and it may make a few new memories!   ☻   Serves 4 (1¼ cups)

> 8 ounces ground 90% lean turkey or beef
> ½ cup chopped onion
> 1¾ cups (one 14½-ounce can) Swanson Beef Broth
> 1¾ cups (3 ounces) uncooked noodles
> 1½ cups frozen cut green beans
> 1½ cups frozen sliced carrots
> ¼ teaspoon black pepper
> 1 (10¾-ounce) can Healthy Request Cream of Mushroom Soup
> 1 teaspoon dried parsley flakes

In a large skillet sprayed with butter-flavored cooking spray, brown meat and onion. Add beef broth. Mix well to combine. Stir in uncooked noodles, green beans, and carrots. Bring mixture to a boil. Lower heat, cover, and simmer for 15 minutes or until noodles and vegetables are tender, stirring occasionally. Stir in black pepper, mushroom soup, and parsley flakes. Continue simmering for 10 minutes or until mixture is heated through, stirring occasionally.

HINT: 1 cup (6 ounces) diced lean cooked roast beef may be used in place of ground meat.

Each serving equals:

> HE: 1¾ Vegetable • 1½ Protein • 1 Bread • ½ Slider •
> 9 Optional Calories
> _____
> 260 Calories • 8 gm Fat • 16 gm Protein •
> 31 gm Carbohydrate • 742 mg Sodium •
> 91 mg Calcium • 3 gm Fiber
> _____
> DIABETIC: 1½ Vegetable • 1½ Meat • 1½ Starch

Tom's Tamale Treat

My son Tommy will always choose Mexican food if he's asked, and now that he lives in the Southwest, he enjoys it all the time. Here's a spicy treat I tested when he was home a while back, and I can happily report he gave it an "A-plus" rating!   ☻   Serves 4

8 ounces ground 90% lean turkey or beef

1/4 cup chopped onion

1 teaspoon chili seasoning

1/4 teaspoon dried minced garlic

1 3/4 cups (one 14 1/2-ounce can) stewed tomatoes, coarsely chopped
    and undrained

2/3 cup Carnation Nonfat Dry Milk Powder

1/2 cup water

1/2 cup (3 ounces) yellow cornmeal

1 cup (one 8-ounce can) cream-style corn

1/4 cup (1 ounce) sliced ripe olives

Preheat oven to 350 degrees. Spray an 8-by-8-inch baking dish with olive oil–flavored cooking spray. In a large skillet sprayed with olive oil–flavored cooking spray, brown meat and onion. Add chili seasoning, garlic, and undrained stewed tomatoes. Mix well to combine. Lower heat and simmer for 5 minutes. In a small bowl, combine dry milk powder and water. Add milk mixture to meat mixture. Mix well to combine. Stir in cornmeal, corn, and olives. Pour mixture into prepared baking dish. Bake for 45 to 50 minutes. Place baking dish on a wire rack and let set for 5 minutes. Divide into 4 servings.

Each serving equals:

HE: 1 1/2 Protein • 1 1/2 Bread • 1 Vegetable •
1/2 Skim Milk • 1/4 Fat

274 Calories • 6 gm Fat • 17 gm Protein •
38 gm Carbohydrate • 687 mg Sodium •
206 mg Calcium • 3 gm Fiber

DIABETIC: 2 Starch/Carbohydrate • 1 1/2 Meat • 1 Vegetable

Skillet Comfort Combo

Whenever there's no time to cook, there's still time to prepare a tasty meal in a skillet in little more than five minutes! This speedy concoction is definitely comfort food made oh-so-easy, so it's a great dish to have in your "meals-on-the-run" repertoire!

○ Serves 6 (1 cup)

16 ounces ground 90% lean turkey or beef
¾ cup chopped onion
1 cup (one 8-ounce can) cream-style corn
1 (10¾-ounce) can Healthy Request Tomato Soup
⅓ cup water
1 teaspoon chili seasoning
1 teaspoon dried parsley flakes
2 cups hot cooked elbow macaroni, rinsed and drained
⅓ cup (1½ ounces) shredded Kraft reduced-fat Cheddar cheese

In a large skillet sprayed with butter-flavored cooking spray, brown meat and onion. Add corn, tomato soup, water, chili seasoning, and parsley flakes. Mix well to combine. Stir in macaroni and Cheddar cheese. Lower heat and simmer for 5 minutes or until mixture is heated through, stirring occasionally.

HINT: 1⅓ cups uncooked elbow macaroni usually cooks to about 2 cups.

Each serving equals:

HE: 2⅓ Protein • 1 Bread • ¼ Vegetable • ¼ Slider • 10 Optional Calories

264 Calories • 8 gm Fat • 19 gm Protein • 29 gm Carbohydrate • 407 mg Sodium • 62 mg Calcium • 2 gm Fiber

DIABETIC: 2 Meat • 1½ Starch

Cheeseburger Turnovers

Here's a dish that used to bring Tommy home to visit, he loved it so much! Your kids will think it's fun to eat cheeseburgers in their own crust instead of on a bun, and your fussy eaters will gobble these down. ☻ Serves 5

4 ounces ground 90% lean turkey or beef

1 tablespoon chopped onion

¼ teaspoon black pepper

½ teaspoon chili seasoning

1 (7.5-ounce) can Pillsbury refrigerated buttermilk biscuits

⅓ cup (1½ ounces) shredded Kraft reduced-fat Cheddar cheese

Preheat oven to 425 degrees. Spray a baking sheet with butter-flavored cooking spray. In a large skillet sprayed with butter-flavored cooking spray, brown meat and onion. Stir in black pepper and chili seasoning. Separate biscuits and place 5 biscuits on prepared baking sheet. Pat each biscuit with hands to form a 4-inch circle. Evenly divide meat mixture over biscuits and sprinkle about 1 tablespoon Cheddar cheese on each. Pat remaining 5 biscuits into 4-inch circles and place over top of meat-filled biscuits. Using the tines of a fork, seal the edges well. Prick top of each 3 or 4 times. Lightly spray tops with butter-flavored cooking spray. Bake for 8 to 10 minutes or until golden brown.

Each serving equals:

HE: 1½ Bread • 1 Protein

156 Calories • 4 gm Fat • 9 gm Protein •
21 gm Carbohydrate • 455 mg Sodium •
55 mg Calcium • 2 gm Fiber

DIABETIC: 1 Starch • 1 Meat

Santa Fe Pizza

Cliff and I drove through New Mexico not long ago, and this recipe is one I created after enjoying such delectable cuisine along the way. Turn up the heat as high as you dare, but mild is wild enough for me—and still scrumptious!　　❂　Serves 8

> 1 (8-ounce) can Pillsbury Reduced Fat Crescent Rolls
> 2 teaspoons cornmeal
> 8 ounces ground 90% lean turkey or beef
> 1¾ cups (one 15-ounce can) stewed tomatoes, coarsely chopped and
> 　　drained
> 1 cup frozen corn, thawed
> ¼ cup chunky salsa (mild, medium, or hot)
> 10 ounces (one 16-ounce can) red kidney beans, rinsed and drained
> 1 tablespoon chili seasoning
> ¾ cup (3 ounces) shredded Kraft reduced-fat Cheddar cheese

Preheat oven to 350 degrees. Pat crescent rolls into an ungreased 10-by-15-inch rimmed baking sheet. Gently press dough to cover bottom of pan, being sure to seal perforations. Lightly spray crust with butter-flavored cooking spray and sprinkle dry cornmeal evenly over top. Bake for 8 to 10 minutes or until golden brown. Place baking sheet on a wire rack and allow to cool. Meanwhile, brown meat in a large skillet sprayed with butter-flavored cooking spray. Add drained stewed tomatoes, corn, salsa, and kidney beans. Mix well to combine. Stir in chili seasoning. Spoon mixture over partially baked crust. Top with Cheddar cheese. Bake for 10 to 12 minutes. Place baking sheet on a wire rack and let set for 5 minutes. Divide into 8 servings.

HINTS: 1. Thaw corn by placing in a colander and rinsing under hot water for one minute.

2. Good topped with 1 tablespoon no-fat sour cream, but don't forget to count the few additional calories.

Each serving equals:

HE: 1¼ Bread • 1¼ Protein • ½ Vegetable • 4 Optional Calories

237 Calories • 9 gm Fat • 13 gm Protein • 26 gm Carbohydrate • 530 mg Sodium • 110 mg Calcium • 3 gm Fiber

DIABETIC: 1½ Starch • 1½ Meat • 1½ Vegetable

No Peek Stew

Few of us have time to watch a pot all day, but now that everyone is unearthing their slow cookers, I've enjoyed creating old-fashioned stews prepared in a smart new way! Now, promise me you won't peek, or all those wonderful flavors will escape when you open the lid too soon! ☻ Serves 8

> 2 pounds extra-lean stew meat
> 1 (10¾-ounce) can Healthy Request Cream of Mushroom Soup
> 1 (1-ounce) package Lipton dry onion soup mix
> 3 cups frozen carrots
> 3 cups frozen cut green beans
> 2½ cups water
> 3½ cups (6 ounces) uncooked noodles

Place stew meat in bottom of a slow cooker container. In a small bowl, combine mushroom soup and dry onion soup mix. Spread soup mixture evenly over meat. Cover and cook on HIGH for 4 hours or until meat is tender. Shortly before serving, in a large saucepan combine carrots, green beans, and water. Bring mixture to a boil. Stir in uncooked noodles. Cook about 15 minutes or until vegetables and noodles are tender. Drain. For each serving, place about ¾ cup noodle mixture on a plate and spoon about ½ cup meat mixture over top.

HINTS: 1. This freezes well, so freeze half of it for another day if it is too much for 1 meal.

2. Cubed lean round steak may be substituted for stew meat.

Each serving equals:

HE: 3 Protein • 1½ Vegetable • 1 Bread •
3 Optional Calories

312 Calories • 8 gm Fat • 30 gm Protein •
30 gm Carbohydrate • 307 mg Sodium •
66 mg Calcium • 4 gm Fiber

DIABETIC: 3 Meat • 1½ Vegetable • 1½ Starch

Roast Beef and Stuffing Bake ❄

If your family likes stuffing so much they could eat it every night, put this recipe on your list to try very soon! It's so easy, so tasty, and thrifty, too, my grandma would be proud.　　●　　Serves 4

½ cup finely chopped onion
1 cup finely chopped celery
1¾ cups (one 14½-ounce can) Swanson Beef Broth ☆
1 teaspoon dried parsley flakes
⅛ teaspoon black pepper
2 cups (3 ounces) purchased herb-seasoned dried bread cubes
1 (10¾-ounce) can Healthy Request Cream of Mushroom Soup
1 full cup (6 ounces) diced lean cooked roast beef

Preheat oven to 350 degrees. Spray an 8-by-8-inch baking dish with butter-flavored cooking spray. In a large skillet sprayed with butter-flavored cooking spray, sauté onion and celery in ½ cup beef broth for 5 minutes or until vegetables are tender. Remove from heat. Stir in remaining 1¼ cups beef broth, parsley flakes, and black pepper. Add bread cubes, mushroom soup, and roast beef. Mix well to combine. Spread mixture into prepared baking dish. Bake for 30 minutes. Place baking dish on a wire rack and let set for 5 minutes. Divide into 4 servings.

HINTS: 1. Pepperidge Farm bread cubes work great.
2. If you don't have leftovers, purchase a chunk of lean cooked roast beef from your local deli or use lean leftover roast pork.

Each serving equals:

HE: 1½ Protein • 1 Bread • ¾ Vegetable • ½ Slider • 10 Optional Calories

204 Calories • 4 gm Fat • 14 gm Protein • 28 gm Carbohydrate • 1292 mg Sodium • 69 mg Calcium • 2 gm Fiber

DIABETIC: 1½ Meat • 1½ Starch

Old Time Pork à la King

If the king of your castle (your husband!) is always asking you to serve pork, here's a man-pleasing dish to delight him! Cliff loves this served over noodles, but you may want to experiment by serving it over rice or toast for a change. ☺ Serves 4 (1 Cup)

> 3 tablespoons all-purpose flour
> 1½ cups (one 12-fluid-ounce can) Carnation Evaporated Skim Milk
> ½ cup (one 2.5-ounce jar) sliced mushrooms, drained
> ¼ cup (one 2-ounce jar) chopped pimiento, drained
> 1 cup frozen peas, thawed
> 1 teaspoon dried parsley flakes
> 1 teaspoon dried onion flakes
> ⅛ teaspoon black pepper
> 1½ cups (8 ounces) diced cooked lean roast pork

In a covered jar, combine flour and evaporated skim milk. Shake well to blend. Pour milk mixture into a medium saucepan sprayed with butter-flavored cooking spray. Cook over medium heat until mixture thickens, stirring constantly. Stir in mushrooms, pimiento, peas, parsley flakes, onion flakes, and black pepper. Add pork. Mix well to combine. Lower heat and simmer for 10 minutes or until mixture is heated through, stirring often.

HINTS: 1. Thaw peas by placing in a colander and rinsing under hot water for one minute.
2. If you don't have leftovers, purchase a chunk of lean cooked roast pork from your local deli.

Each serving equals:

HE: 2 Protein • ¾ Bread • ¾ Skim Milk • ¼ Vegetable

285 Calories • 9 gm Fat • 27 gm Protein •
24 gm Carbohydrate • 259 mg Sodium •
337 mg Calcium • 3 gm Fiber

DIABETIC: 2 Meat • 1 Starch • 1 Skim Milk

Pork-n-Rice Skillet

Maybe you never knew for sure how your grandma made her delectable gravies or just what secret ingredients went into her sauces, but I'm happy to share all I know! It's amazing to see just what happens when ketchup and mustard hold hands in this cozy dish.

🄾 Serves 4 (1 full cup)

½ cup chopped onion
1¾ cups (one 14½-ounce can) Swanson Beef Broth
1⅓ cups (4 ounces) uncooked Minute Rice
1 teaspoon prepared mustard
2 cups (one 16-ounce can) tomatoes, coarsely chopped and
*   undrained*
¼ cup Heinz Light Harvest Ketchup or any reduced-sodium ketchup
1 teaspoon dried parsley flakes
½ cup chopped green bell pepper
1½ cups (8 ounces) diced cooked lean roast pork

In a large skillet sprayed with butter-flavored cooking spray, sauté onion for 5 minutes or until tender. Stir in beef broth, uncooked rice, and mustard. Bring mixture to a boil. Add undrained tomatoes, ketchup, parsley flakes, and green pepper. Mix well to combine. Lower heat and simmer for 20 minutes, stirring occasionally. Add pork. Mix well to combine. Continue simmering for 5 minutes or until mixture is heated through, stirring often.

HINT: If you don't have leftovers, purchase a chunk of cooked lean roast pork from your local deli.

Each serving equals:

HE: 2 Protein • 1½ Vegetable • 1 Bread •
18 Optional Calories

216 Calories • 4 gm Fat • 17 gm Protein •
28 gm Carbohydrate • 578 mg Sodium •
56 mg Calcium • 2 gm Fiber

DIABETIC: 3 Meat • 1 Vegetable • 1 Starch

Skillet Ham Hash

This dish is a great quick meal to satisfy the entire family, and the flour does its thickening trick to make a luscious gravy. Topped with a tasty reduced-fat cheese that melts so beautifully and tastes so good, this recipe works wonders with hungry kids.   ☻   Serves 4 (1 cup)

½ cup chopped onion

2 cups (12 ounces) diced cooked potatoes

1 full cup (6 ounces) diced Dubuque 97% fat-free ham or any extra-lean ham

½ cup (one 2.5-ounce jar) sliced mushrooms, drained

⅓ cup Carnation Nonfat Dry Milk Powder

½ cup water

1 tablespoon all-purpose flour

1 teaspoon dried parsley flakes

⅛ teaspoon black pepper

4 (¾-ounce) slices Kraft reduced-fat Swiss cheese, shredded

In a large skillet sprayed with butter-flavored cooking spray, sauté onion for 5 minutes or until tender. Add potatoes, ham, and mushrooms. Mix well to combine. In a covered jar, combine dry milk powder, water, flour, parsley flakes, and black pepper. Shake well to blend. Stir milk mixture into potato mixture. Lower heat and simmer for 10 minutes, stirring often. Add Swiss cheese. Mix well to combine. Continue simmering for 3 to 5 minutes or until cheese melts, stirring occasionally.

Each serving equals:

HE: 2 Protein • ¾ Bread • ¼ Skim Milk • ¼ Vegetable • 8 Optional Calories

138 Calories • 2 gm Fat • 13 gm Protein • 17 gm Carbohydrate • 449 mg Sodium • 254 mg Calcium • 1 gm Fiber

DIABETIC: 1½ Meat • 1 Starch

Ham and Cheese Casserole ❄

Why not take a favorite sandwich and turn it into an even more delicious main dish? That was my thought when I began choosing ingredients for this flavorful recipe, and Cliff agreed that I'd improved on the original! I hope you do, too. ☻ Serves 4

3 tablespoons all-purpose flour
1½ cups (one 12-fluid-ounce can) Carnation Evaporated Skim Milk
⅛ teaspoon black pepper
¾ cup (3 ounces) shredded Kraft reduced-fat Cheddar cheese
1½ cups hot cooked noodles, rinsed and drained
1 cup (one 8-ounce can) cut green beans, rinsed and drained
1 full cup (6 ounces) diced Dubuque 97% fat-free ham or any extra-lean ham

Preheat oven to 350 degrees. Spray an 8-by-8-inch baking dish with butter-flavored cooking spray. In a covered jar, combine flour, evaporated skim milk, and black pepper. Shake well to blend. Pour milk mixture into a medium saucepan sprayed with butter-flavored cooking spray. Stir in Cheddar cheese. Cook over medium heat until sauce thickens, stirring constantly. Add noodles, green beans, and ham. Mix well to combine. Spoon mixture into prepared baking dish. Bake for 20 minutes. Place baking dish on a wire rack and let set for 5 minutes. Divide into 4 servings.

HINTS: 1. 1¼ cups uncooked noodles usually cooks to about 1½ cups.

    2. Thaw peas by placing in a colander and rinsing under hot water for one minute.

Each serving equals:

HE: 2 Protein • 1 Bread • ¾ Skim Milk • ½ Vegetable

290 Calories • 6 gm Fat • 24 gm Protein •
35 gm Carbohydrate • 654 mg Sodium •
443 mg Calcium • 2 gm Fiber

DIABETIC: 1½ Meat • 1½ Starch • 1 Skim Milk •
½ Vegetable

Ham and Beans Duo

Simple ingredients, simple techniques—that's what it takes to prepare comfort food that really satisfies! If ever a recipe proved that point, it's this one, which starts with the basics and just lets them cook together, melding their unique flavors into one terrific dish.

○ Serves 4 (full ½ cup)

> 1 full cup (6 ounces) diced Dubuque 97% fat-free ham or any extra-
> lean ham
> ½ cup chopped onion
> 10 ounces (one 16-ounce can) great northern beans, rinsed and
> drained
> ¼ cup water
> ¼ teaspoon lemon pepper

In a large skillet sprayed with butter-flavored cooking spray, sauté ham and onion for 5 minutes or until onion is tender. Add great northern beans, water, and lemon pepper. Mix well to combine. Lower heat, cover, and simmer for 10 minutes, stirring occasionally.

Each serving equals:

HE: 2¼ Protein • ¼ Vegetable

---

138 Calories • 2 gm Fat • 13 gm Protein •
17 gm Carbohydrate • 362 mg Sodium •
52 mg Calcium • 4 gm Fiber

DIABETIC: 2 Meat • 1 Starch

Ham–Sweet Potato–Apple Dish ❄

Do you or your kids have a true sweet tooth, even when it comes to entrees? This might be the recipe with your name on it! I've combined the natural goodness of sweet potatoes and ham with a variety of fruits, then baked it all together in the microwave with a touch of nuts and maple. As Jackie Gleason used to say, "How sweet it is!"

◑ Serves 4 (1 full cup)

> *2 full cups (12 ounces) diced cooked sweet potatoes or yams*
> *1 cup (2 small) cored, unpeeled, and chopped cooking apples*
> *½ cup (3 ounces) chopped dried apricots*
> *2 tablespoons raisins*
> *¼ cup Cary's Sugar Free Maple Syrup*
> *2 tablespoons (½ ounce) chopped pecans*
> *1 full cup (6 ounces) diced Dubuque 97% fat-free ham or any extra-lean ham*

In an 8-cup glass measuring bowl, combine sweet potatoes, apples, apricots, and raisins. Stir in maple syrup. Cover and microwave on HIGH (100% power) for 6 to 7 minutes. Add pecans and ham. Mix well to combine. Continue microwaving on HIGH for 5 minutes. Let set 2 to 3 minutes. Mix well before serving.

Each serving equals:

HE: 1¾ Fruit • 1 Bread • 1 Protein • ½ Fat • 10 Optional Calories

236 Calories • 4 gm Fat • 10 gm Protein • 40 gm Carbohydrate • 442 mg Sodium • 34 mg Calcium • 6 gm Fiber

DIABETIC: 1½ Fruit • 1 Starch • 1 Meat • ½ Fat

Creamed Chipped Beef and Rice Skillet

Cliff has always loved this trucker's favorite, and so I've come up with lots of ways to prepare it. This is a remarkably creamy dish, and oh, when that rice soaks up the sauce, you'll really believe it's a taste of old-timey heaven! ☻ Serves 4 (1 cup)

> 1 (4.5-ounce) jar Hormel reduced-fat chipped beef, rinsed, drained, and shredded
> 3 tablespoons all-purpose flour
> 2 cups skim milk
> 1 (8-ounce) package Philadelphia fat-free cream cheese
> 1½ cups hot cooked rice
> 2 cups (one 16-ounce can) cut green beans, rinsed and drained
> ⅛ teaspoon black pepper
> ½ teaspoon dried parsley flakes

In a large skillet sprayed with butter-flavored cooking spray, brown chipped beef. In a covered jar, combine flour and skim milk. Shake well to blend. Pour milk mixture over chipped beef. Mix well to combine. Stir in cream cheese. Continue cooking until cheese melts, stirring often. Add rice, green beans, black pepper, and parsley flakes. Mix well to combine. Lower heat and simmer for 10 minutes or until mixture is heated through, stirring often.

HINT: 1 cup uncooked rice usually cooks to about 1½ cups.

Each serving equals:

> HE: 2 Protein • 1 Bread • 1 Vegetable • ½ Skim Milk •
> 8 Optional Calories
> _____
> 221 Calories • 1 gm Fat • 22 gm Protein •
> 31 gm Carbohydrate • 737 mg Sodium •
> 176 mg Calcium • 2 gm Fiber
> _____
> DIABETIC: 2 Meat • 1½ Starch • ½ Skim Milk

Golden Frankfurter Skillet ❄

This is the kind of skillet supper Josh and Zach, my grandbabies, just love "Gamma" to make! It's so cozy-warm, so creamy and cheesy good, and features their beloved hot dogs—you never saw two better-behaved little boys on nights I'm serving this!

◐ Serves 4 (1 cup)

8 ounces Healthy Choice 97% fat-free frankfurters, diced
1 (10¾-ounce) can Healthy Choice Cream of Mushroom Soup
¾ cup (3 ounces) shredded Kraft reduced-fat Cheddar cheese
⅓ cup skim milk
½ cup (one 2.5-ounce jar) sliced mushrooms, drained
1½ cups hot cooked noodles, rinsed and drained
½ cup frozen whole-kernel corn, thawed
1 teaspoon dried parsley flakes
¼ teaspoon black pepper

In a large skillet sprayed with butter-flavored cooking spray, sauté frankfurters for 5 minutes. Stir in mushroom soup, Cheddar cheese, and skim milk. Continue cooking until cheese melts, stirring often. Add mushrooms, noodles, corn, parsley flakes, and black pepper. Mix well to combine. Lower heat and simmer for 5 minutes, or until mixture is heated through, stirring occasionally.

HINTS: 1. 1¼ cups uncooked noodles usually cooks to about 1½ cups.
2. Thaw corn by placing in a colander and rinsing under hot water for one minute.

Each serving equals:

HE: 2⅓ Protein • 1 Bread • ¼ Vegetable • ½ Slider • 10 Optional Calories

271 Calories • 7 gm Fat • 19 gm Protein •
33 gm Carbohydrate • 1169 mg Sodium •
240 mg Calcium • 2 gm Fiber

DIABETIC: 2 Meat • 2 Starch/Carbohydrate

Polish Sausage and Kraut Stew

This is such a perfect example of a recipe no one believes could ever be healthy, but I'm delighted to prove that it is! This dish is my way of saying thanks to those wonderful sausage makers who gave us a lean version of this beloved Polish sausage. And because I'm such a fan of sauerkraut, I love combining these two favorites in a hearty stew.

♥   Serves 6 (1⅓ cups)

> 16 ounces Healthy Choice 97% lean kielbasa sausage, cut into
>   ½-inch pieces
> 2 cups water
> 1 (10¾-ounce) can Healthy Request Cream of Mushroom Soup
> 1¾ cups (one 14½-ounce can) Frank's Bavarian style sauerkraut,
>   drained
> 3 cups (20 ounces) peeled and diced raw potatoes
> ¾ cup chopped onion
> 1 cup sliced carrots
> ½ cup chopped celery

In a medium saucepan, combine sausage and water. Bring mixture to a boil. Drain. In a slow cooker container, combine mushroom soup and sauerkraut. Add potatoes, onion, carrots, and celery. Mix well to combine. Stir in sausage. Cover and cook on LOW for 8 hours. Mix well before serving.

HINT: If you can't find Bavarian sauerkraut, use regular sauerkraut, ½ teaspoon caraway seeds, and 1 teaspoon Brown Sugar Twin.

Each serving equals:

HE: 1¾ Protein • 1⅓ Vegetable • ½ Bread • ¼ Slider • 8 Optional Calories

204 Calories • 4 gm Fat • 16 gm Protein • 26 gm Carbohydrate • 988 mg Sodium • 72 mg Calcium • 4 gm Fiber

DIABETIC: 2 Meat • 1½ Vegetable • 1½ Starch

Bountiful Harvest Stew

Here's another tasty treat that stars kielbasa, then invites it to dance with the best of the fall harvest—sweet potatoes, apples, and more! What better way to celebrate the Lord's bounty than to serve it to the people we love best—our families! ❂ Serves 4 (1½ cups)

> 2 cups (one 16-ounce can) Healthy Request Chicken Broth
> 1 tablespoon prepared mustard
> 3 full cups (16 ounces) peeled and thinly sliced raw sweet potatoes
> ½ cup coarsely chopped onion
> 8 ounces Healthy Choice 97% lean kielbasa sausage, cut into thin
>   slices
> 4 cups coarsely shredded cabbage
> 1 cup (2 small) unpeeled, cored, and coarsely chopped Red
>   Delicious apples

In a large skillet, combine chicken broth and mustard. Bring mixture to a boil. Add sweet potatoes and onion. Lower heat, cover, and simmer for 10 minutes, stirring occasionally. Add sausage and cabbage. Mix well to combine. Cover and continue cooking for 20 minutes or until potatoes and cabbage are tender, stirring occasionally. Stir in apples. Continue simmering for 5 minutes or until apples are just tender, stirring occasionally.

Each serving equals:

HE: 2¼ Vegetable • 1½ Protein • 1 Bread • ½ Fruit •
8 Optional Calories

223 Calories • 3 gm Fat • 14 gm Protein •
35 gm Carbohydrate • 808 mg Sodium •
61 mg Calcium • 5 gm Fiber

DIABETIC: 2 Meat • 1 Vegetable • 1 Starch • ½ Fruit

Desserts

Didn't it seem as if something was always baking in your grandmother's oven? That there was an endless supply of mouthwatering cookies, luscious cakes, creamy puddings, and golden-crusted pies bursting with fruit? My grandma cooked over a wood-burning stove, and every time I visited, I'd put on my apron and help her stir up a tantalizing variety of baked goods.

From her, I learned so much of what I know about preparing scrumptious desserts of all kinds. She taught me how to roll out a piecrust and slice apples for pie; she shared her secrets for making meringues that wouldn't tumble in the oven and cakes that emerged from the oven beautifully browned but never dry or overdone. Most of all, she gave me a deep appreciation for the role a lovingly prepared dessert plays in our lives.

Lots of people tell me that when they buy one of my cookbooks, they always turn to the dessert section first! If you headed here first, I know you'll find yourself wondering which of these irresistible recipes to stir up today. Hmm— will it be my Mile-High Chocolate Fruit Pie, or perhaps a Moist Apple Caramel Cake? Maybe you'll choose one of Cliff's favorites, my Banana Split Dessert Pizza. I promise you this: Whatever you choose, your family will cheer!

Desserts

Creamy Apricot Rice Pudding

Rice pudding was always a favorite at my grandma's boardinghouse, and I've never lost my childhood love for its cool and creamy joys! I thought apricots would be a nice addition to the traditional ingredients, along with just a few of my favorite nuts: pecans.

◑ Serves 6

1½ cups water

1⅓ cups (4 ounces) uncooked Minute Rice

½ cup (3 ounces) chopped dried apricots

¼ cup Sugar Twin or Sprinkle Sweet ☆

2 tablespoons (½ ounce) chopped pecans

¾ cup Yoplait plain fat-free yogurt

⅓ cup Carnation Nonfat Dry Milk Powder

1 teaspoon vanilla extract

¾ cup Cool Whip Free

In a medium saucepan, bring water to a boil. Stir in uncooked rice, apricots, and 2 tablespoons Sugar Twin. Cover and simmer for 5 minutes. Remove from heat. Let set, covered, about 5 minutes or until all water is absorbed. Stir in pecans. Spoon rice mixture into a large bowl and refrigerate for at least 30 minutes. In a small bowl, combine yogurt and dry milk powder. Stir in vanilla extract, remaining 2 tablespoons Sugar Twin, and Cool Whip Free. Add yogurt mixture to rice mixture. Mix well to combine. Evenly spoon mixture into 6 dessert dishes. Refrigerate for at least 30 minutes.

Each serving equals:

HE: ⅔ Fruit • ⅔ Bread • ⅓ Skim Milk • ⅓ Fat •
¼ Slider • 1 Optional Calorie

154 Calories • 2 gm Fat • 5 gm Protein •
29 gm Carbohydrate • 50 mg Sodium •
114 mg Calcium • 3 gm Fiber

DIABETIC: 1½ Starch/Carbohydrate • ½ Fruit • ½ Fat
or 2 Starch/Carbohydrate • 1 Fat

Yesteryear Applesauce-Rice Pudding

It's almost like a perfect child's fantasy—combining a favorite dessert like rice pudding with some luscious applesauce! And finding those plump raisins hidden in each serving is my favorite kind of culinary treasure hunt. ☺ Serves 6

> 1 (4-serving) package JELL-O sugar-free instant vanilla pudding mix
> ⅔ cup Carnation Nonfat Dry Milk Powder
> 1 cup water
> 1 cup unsweetened applesauce
> ½ cup Cool Whip Free
> ½ teaspoon apple pie spice
> 2 cups cold cooked rice
> ¼ cup raisins

In a large bowl, combine dry pudding mix, dry milk powder, and water. Mix well using a wire whisk. Stir in applesauce, Cool Whip Free, and apple pie spice. Add rice and raisins. Mix well to combine. Evenly spoon mixture into 6 dessert dishes. Refrigerate for at least 30 minutes.

HINTS: 1. To plump up raisins without "cooking," place in a glass measuring cup and microwave on HIGH for 20 seconds.

2. 1⅓ cups uncooked rice usually cooks to about 2 cups.

Each serving equals:

HE: ⅔ Fruit • ⅔ Bread • ⅓ Skim Milk •
10 Optional Calories

152 Calories • 0 gm Fat • 4 gm Protein •
34 gm Carbohydrate • 256 mg Sodium •
101 mg Calcium • 1 gm Fiber

DIABETIC: 1 Fruit • 1 Starch/Carbohydrate

Mandarin Tapioca Pudding

Tapioca is a wonderful, old-fashioned dessert dear to my husband's heart, so this is a taste treat created with Cliff in mind. The intense orange flavor provided by the gelatin as well as the fruit makes this especially irresistible!   ❤   Serves 4

> 1 (4-serving) package JELL-O sugar-free vanilla cook-and-serve pudding mix
>
> 1 (4-serving) package JELL-O sugar-free orange gelatin
>
> 3 tablespoons Quick Cooking Minute Tapioca
>
> ⅔ cup Carnation Nonfat Dry Milk Powder
>
> 2 cups water
>
> 1 cup (one 11-ounce can) mandarin oranges, rinsed and drained

In a large saucepan, combine dry pudding mix, dry gelatin, dry tapioca, dry milk powder, and water. Let set 5 minutes. Cook over medium heat until mixture thickens and starts to boil, stirring often. Remove from heat. Stir in mandarin oranges. Evenly spoon mixture into 4 dessert dishes. Refrigerate for at least 30 minutes.

Each serving equals:

HE: ½ Fruit • ½ Skim Milk • ½ Slider •
13 Optional Calories

120 Calories • 0 gm Fat • 6 gm Protein •
24 gm Carbohydrate • 235 mg Sodium •
159 mg Calcium • 0 gm Fiber

DIABETIC: 1½ Starch/Carbohydrate

Banana Raisin Custard

Remember when you were sick in bed and your mom or grandma served you custard, so smooth and creamy that you found you had an appetite after all? This is a dessert worth taking to your bed for, but luckily you don't have to—you can just stir it up anytime and enjoy it with YOUR kids! ☻ Serves 4

> 1 cup (1 medium) diced banana
> 1 (4-serving) package JELL-O sugar-free vanilla cook-and-serve pudding mix
> ⅔ cup Carnation Nonfat Dry Milk Powder
> 1¾ cups water
> ¼ cup raisins
> 1 teaspoon vanilla extract
> ¼ cup Cool Whip Lite
> Dash ground cinnamon

Evenly divide banana among 4 custard cups. In a medium saucepan, combine dry pudding mix, dry milk powder, and water. Add raisins. Mix well to combine. Cook over medium heat until mixture thickens and starts to boil, stirring constantly. Remove from heat. Stir in vanilla extract. Evenly spoon hot pudding mixture into custard cups. Refrigerate for at least 2 hours. When serving, top each with 1 tablespoon Cool Whip Lite and a light sprinkling of cinnamon.

HINT: To prevent banana from turning brown, mix with 1 teaspoon lemon juice or sprinkle with Fruit Fresh.

Each serving equals:

HE: 1 Fruit • ½ Skim Milk • ¼ Slider •
15 Optional Calories

145 Calories • 1 gm Fat • 5 gm Protein •
29 gm Carbohydrate • 394 mg Sodium •
157 mg Calcium • 1 gm Fiber

DIABETIC: 1 Fruit • 1 Starch/Carbohydrate *or*
1 Fruit • ½ Skim Milk • ½ Starch/Carbohydrate

Tea Time Fruit Dessert

This is so beautiful, it's almost a shame to cut it and serve it—but you will, of course! It's just too good to resist. Here, I'm using one of my favorite "instant-crust" techniques, arranging graham crackers in the bottom of a baking pan to create a homemade crust that couldn't be simpler!   ☻   Serves 8

> 12 (2½-inch) graham cracker squares ☆
> 1 cup (one 8-ounce can) crushed pineapple, packed in fruit juice,
>   drained, and ¼ cup liquid reserved
> 2 cups (one 16-ounce can) tart red cherries, packed in water,
>   drained, and ½ cup liquid reserved
> ¾ cup water
> 1 (4-serving) package JELL-O sugar-free vanilla cook-and-serve pud-
>   ding mix
> 1 (4-serving) package JELL-O sugar-free raspberry gelatin
> 2 tablespoons (½ ounce) chopped pecans
> 1 cup (1 medium) diced banana
> 1 cup Cool Whip Lite

Arrange 9 graham crackers in a 9-by-9-inch cake pan. In a medium saucepan, combine reserved pineapple and cherry liquids, water, dry pudding mix, and dry gelatin. Stir in pineapple and cherries. Mix gently to combine. Cook over medium heat until mixture thickens and starts to boil, stirring constantly, and being careful not to crush fruit. Remove from heat. Stir in pecans and banana. Let set for 10 minutes. Evenly spoon mixture over crackers. Refrigerate for at least 2 hours or until firm. Spread Cool Whip Lite evenly over set filling. Crush remaining 3 graham crackers into crumbs. Evenly sprinkle cracker crumbs over top. Cut into 8 servings.

HINT: A self-seal sandwich bag works great for crushing graham
      crackers.

Each serving equals:

HE: 1 Fruit • ½ Bread • ¼ Fat • ¼ Slider • 15 Optional Calories

131 Calories • 3 gm Fat • 2 gm Protein • 24 gm Carbohydrate • 124 mg Sodium • 13 mg Calcium • 1 gm Fiber

DIABETIC: 1 Fruit • ½ Starch/Carbohydrate • ½ Fat

Layered Berry Fruit Dessert

If you're planning a Fourth of July party and you want your dessert to be the featured attraction, serve this truly festive dish! I love using the freshest berries from the farmers' market, but I've also made this when my favorite berries just weren't in season, by substituting frozen ones. Let the fireworks begin!   ◑   Serves 8

27 (2½-inch) graham cracker squares
1¾ cups water ☆
1 (4-serving) package JELL-O sugar-free lemon gelatin
3 cups fresh blueberries
2 (8-ounce) packages Philadelphia fat-free cream cheese
1 teaspoon vanilla extract
Sugar substitute to equal 2 tablespoons sugar
1 cup Cool Whip Free
1 (4-serving) package JELL-O sugar-free raspberry gelatin
1½ cups fresh red raspberries

Evenly arrange 9 of the graham crackers in a 9-by-9-inch cake pan. In a medium saucepan, combine 1 cup water and dry lemon gelatin. Cook over medium heat until gelatin dissolves, stirring constantly. Stir in blueberries. Continue cooking for 1 to 2 minutes longer, being careful not to crush blueberries. Spoon hot mixture over crackers. Evenly arrange another 9 crackers over top. In a medium bowl, stir cream cheese with a spoon until soft. Add vanilla extract, sugar substitute, and Cool Whip Free. Mix well to combine. Spread mixture evenly over crackers. Arrange another 9 crackers over cream cheese mixture. In a medium saucepan, combine remaining ¾ cup water and dry raspberry gelatin. Cook over medium heat until gelatin dissolves, stirring constantly. Stir in raspberries. Continue cooking for 1 to 2 minutes longer, being careful not to crush raspberries. Spoon raspberry mixture evenly over crackers. Refrigerate for at least 2 hours. Cut into 8 servings.

HINT: Frozen, unsweetened fruit, thawed and well drained, may be substituted for fresh.

Each serving equals:

HE: 1 Bread • 1 Protein • ¾ Fruit • ¼ Slider •
17 Optional Calories

207 Calories • 3 gm Fat • 12 gm Protein •
33 gm Carbohydrate • 515 mg Sodium •
79 mg Calcium • 2 gm Fiber

DIABETIC: 1½ Starch/Carbohydrate • 1 Meat • 1 Fruit

Orange-Pineapple Dream Pie

I think I had my eyes closed when I first saw this pie in my mind's eye—and I knew immediately it was a winner! It's the colors of a summer sunset, and it's so rich and sweet you'll wonder if you're in Fantasyland. Wake up—you're enjoying a healthy pie, and isn't it great!

◐ Serves 8

1 (4-serving) package JELL-O sugar-free vanilla cook-and-serve pudding mix
⅔ cup Carnation Nonfat Dry Milk Powder
1 cup unsweetened orange juice
¾ cup water
½ teaspoon coconut extract
1 cup (one 8-ounce can) crushed pineapple, packed in fruit juice, drained
½ cup (1 ounce) miniature marshmallows
1 (6-ounce) Keebler graham cracker piecrust
½ cup Cool Whip Lite
4 teaspoons flaked coconut

In a medium saucepan, combine dry pudding mix, dry milk powder, orange juice, and water. Cook over medium heat until mixture thickens and starts to boil, stirring constantly with a wire whisk. Remove from heat. Stir in coconut extract. Place saucepan on a wire rack and let set for 5 minutes. Add pineapple and marshmallows. Mix gently to combine. Spread mixture into piecrust. Refrigerate for at least 2 hours. Cut into 8 servings. When serving, top each piece with 1 tablespoon Cool Whip Lite and garnish with ½ teaspoon coconut.

Each serving equals:

HE: ½ Fruit • ½ Bread • ¼ Skim Milk • ¾ Slider • 19 Optional Calories

---

182 Calories • 6 gm Fat • 2 gm Protein • 30 gm Carbohydrate • 213 mg Sodium • 45 mg Calcium • 1 gm Fiber

---

DIABETIC: 1½ Starch/Carbohydrate • 1 Fat • ½ Fruit

Sparkling Fruit Pie

Strawberries by the pint always call my name when I'm at the store or the farm stand, and when I find myself with a bowl of fresh berries, I put on my recipe-creating cap and keep discovering wonderful new ways to feature this gem of all fruits. I especially love this one because the strawberry taste is extra-intense.

◐ Serves 8

> 2 cups (2 medium) diced bananas
> 2 cups sliced fresh strawberries
> 1 (6-ounce) Keebler shortbread piecrust
> 1 (4-serving) package JELL-O sugar-free vanilla cook-and-serve pudding mix
> 1 (4-serving) package JELL-O sugar-free strawberry gelatin
> 1½ cups Diet Sprite or Diet 7UP
> ½ cup Cool Whip Lite

In a large bowl, combine bananas and strawberries. Spoon fruit into piecrust. In a medium saucepan, combine dry pudding mix, dry gelatin, and Diet Sprite. Cook over medium heat until mixture thickens and starts to boil, stirring often. Pour hot mixture evenly over fruit. Refrigerate for at least 2 hours. Cut into 8 servings. When serving, top each piece with 1 tablespoon Cool Whip Lite.

HINT: To prevent bananas from turning brown, mix with 1 teaspoon lemon juice or sprinkle with Fruit Fresh.

Each serving equals:

HE: ¾ Fruit • ½ Bread • ¾ Slider •
15 Optional Calories

182 Calories • 6 gm Fat • 2 gm Protein •
30 gm Carbohydrate • 333 mg Sodium •
7 mg Calcium • 2 gm Fiber

DIABETIC: 1 Fruit • 1 Starch/Carbohydrate • 1 Fat

Mile-High Chocolate Fruit Pie

Just the name tells you how special this recipe is! As you pile the layers ever higher, and you add more wonderful flavors to this luscious pie, imagine your family's reaction to such a terrific treat—and you might want to rename it "Smile-High Chocolate Fruit Pie"!

☻ Serves 8

1 cup (1 medium) sliced banana
1 (6-ounce) Keebler graham cracker piecrust
1 (4-serving) package JELL-O sugar-free instant chocolate pudding
    mix
⅔ cup Carnation Nonfat Dry Milk Powder
1¼ cups water
2 cups finely chopped fresh strawberries
1 (8-ounce) package Philadelphia fat-free cream cheese
1 cup Cool Whip Free
Sugar substitute to equal 1 tablespoon sugar
½ teaspoon vanilla extract
8 teaspoons Hershey's Lite Chocolate Syrup

Layer banana in bottom of piecrust. In a medium bowl, combine dry pudding mix, dry milk powder, and water. Mix well using a wire whisk. Pour mixture over banana. Refrigerate for 5 minutes. Arrange strawberries over set filling. In a medium bowl, stir cream cheese with a spoon until soft. Add Cool Whip Free, sugar substitute, and vanilla extract. Mix well to blend. Spread topping mixture evenly over strawberries. Refrigerate for at least 2 hours. Cut into 8 servings. When serving, drizzle 1 teaspoon chocolate syrup over each piece.

HINT: To prevent banana from turning brown, mix with 1 teaspoon lemon juice or sprinkle with Fruit Fresh.

Each serving equals:

HE: ½ Bread • ½ Fruit • ½ Protein • ¼ Skim Milk •
1 Slider • 11 Optional Calories

---

221 Calories • 5 gm Fat • 8 gm Protein •
36 gm Carbohydrate • 512 mg Sodium •
77 mg Calcium • 2 gm Fiber

DIABETIC: 1½ Starch/Carbohydrate • 1 Fruit • ½ Meat •
½ Fat

Lemon Cream Pie with Raspberry Glaze

Are you invited to a summer bridal shower and can't decide what dessert to bring? Here's one that gets my vote, an elegant tart and creamy lemon dessert topped with a glorious glaze! Best wishes to the bride, but at least your lips and your hips are sure to live happily ever after. . . .   ◯   Serves 8

1 (4-serving) package JELL-O sugar-free instant vanilla pudding mix

1 (4-serving) package JELL-O sugar-free lemon gelatin

⅔ cup Carnation Nonfat Dry Milk Powder

1¼ cups Diet Mountain Dew ☆

1 cup Cool Whip Lite ☆

1 (6-ounce) Keebler shortbread piecrust

1 (4-serving) package JELL-O sugar-free raspberry gelatin

1½ cups unsweetened red raspberries, fresh or frozen, thawed

In a medium bowl, combine dry pudding mix, dry lemon gelatin, dry milk powder, and ¾ cup Diet Mountain Dew. Mix well using a wire whisk. Blend in ½ cup Cool Whip Lite. Spread mixture into piecrust. Refrigerate while preparing glaze. In a medium saucepan, combine remaining ½ cup Diet Mountain Dew and dry raspberry gelatin. Cook over medium heat until gelatin dissolves, stirring constantly. Stir in raspberries and continue cooking for 1 to 2 minutes longer, stirring often and being careful not to crush berries. Remove from heat. Place saucepan on a wire rack and allow to cool for 10 minutes. Spread raspberry mixture evenly over lemon filling. Refrigerate for at least 2 hours. Cut into 8 servings. When serving, top each piece with 1 tablespoon Cool Whip Lite.

Each serving equals:

HE: ½ Bread • ¼ Skim Milk • ¼ Fruit • 1 Slider • 13 Optional Calories

177 Calories • 5 gm Fat • 5 gm Protein • 28 gm Carbohydrate • 390 mg Sodium • 76 mg Calcium • 2 gm Fiber

DIABETIC: 2 Starch/Carbohydrate • ½ Fat

Heavenly Mandarin Orange Cream Pie

There's just something magical about the combination of chocolate and orange, and when your loved ones taste this lovely treat, they're sure to be convinced that you've been touched by an angel!

♥ Serves 8

> 1 (4-serving) package JELL-O sugar-free instant vanilla pudding mix
>
> 1 (4-serving) package JELL-O sugar-free orange gelatin
>
> ⅔ cup Carnation Nonfat Dry Milk Powder
>
> 1 cup Diet Mountain Dew
>
> 1 cup Cool Whip Lite ☆
>
> 1 teaspoon coconut extract
>
> 2 cups (two 11-ounce cans) mandarin oranges, rinsed and drained
>
> 1 (6-ounce) Keebler chocolate piecrust
>
> 4 teaspoons Hershey's Lite Chocolate Syrup
>
> 4 teaspoons flaked coconut

In a large bowl, combine dry pudding mix, dry gelatin, dry milk powder, and Diet Mountain Dew. Mix well using a wire whisk. Blend in ½ cup Cool Whip Lite and coconut extract. Add oranges. Mix gently to combine. Spread mixture into piecrust. Refrigerate for at least 2 hours. Cut into 8 servings. When serving, top each piece with 1 tablespoon Cool Whip Lite, drizzle ½ teaspoon chocolate syrup over top and garnish with ½ teaspoon coconut.

Each serving equals:

> HE: ½ Fruit • ½ Bread • ¼ Skim Milk • 1 Slider • 16 Optional Calories
>
> ---
>
> 194 Calories • 6 gm Fat • 4 gm Protein • 31 gm Carbohydrate • 331 mg Sodium • 76 mg Calcium • 1 gm Fiber
>
> ---
>
> DIABETIC: 2 Starch/Carbohydrate • ½ Fat

Grandma's Peanut Butter Pie ❄

This is a perfect pie for the very next bake sale you contribute to, and I'll tell you why: No one can pass by a perfect peanut butter pie! Especially not one as appealing as this one, with its drizzled chocolate and caramel toppings . . . ○ Serves 8

> 1 (4-serving) package JELL-O sugar-free instant vanilla pudding mix
> ⅔ cup Carnation Nonfat Dry Milk Powder
> 1⅓ cups water
> 6 tablespoons Peter Pan reduced-fat chunky peanut butter
> 1 cup Cool Whip Free ☆
> 1 (6-ounce) Keebler graham cracker piecrust
> 2 teaspoons Hershey's Lite Chocolate Syrup
> 2 teaspoons caramel syrup

In a large mixing bowl, combine dry pudding mix, dry milk powder, and water. Mix well using a wire whisk. Blend in peanut butter and ½ cup Cool Whip Free. Pour mixture into piecrust. Refrigerate for at least 15 minutes. Spread remaining ½ cup Cool Whip Free over set filling. Just before serving, drizzle chocolate syrup and caramel syrup over top. Cut into 8 servings.

Each serving equals:

HE: ¾ Protein • ¾ Fat • ½ Bread • ¼ Skim Milk •
1 Slider

225 Calories • 9 gm Fat • 6 gm Protein •
30 gm Carbohydrate • 399 mg Sodium •
70 mg Calcium • 1 gm Fiber

DIABETIC: 2 Starch/Carbohydrate • 1 Fat • ½ Meat

Rhubarb Pie with "Brown Sugar" Meringue

Rhubarb in all its glory is a Midwestern classic, and never more when it's baked into a beautiful pie like this one! If you've never made a meringue, you'll be surprised how easy it is when you follow my simple directions. Then just stand back and enjoy the compliments you get from everywhere! ☻ Serves 8

1 Pillsbury refrigerated unbaked 9-inch piecrust
2 (4-serving) packages JELL-O sugar-free vanilla cook-and-serve
    pudding mixes
1⅓ cups water
¼ teaspoon ground nutmeg
4 cups finely diced fresh rhubarb
6 egg whites
6 tablespoons Sugar Twin or Sprinkle Sweet
2 tablespoons Brown Sugar Twin
1 teaspoon vanilla extract

Preheat oven to 450 degrees. Place piecrust in a 9-inch pie plate. Flute edges and prick bottom and sides with the tines of a fork. Bake for 6 to 8 minutes or until lightly browned. Place pie plate on a wire rack and allow to cool completely. Meanwhile, lower oven temperature to 350 degrees. In a large saucepan, combine dry pudding mixes, water, and nutmeg. Stir in rhubarb. Cook over medium heat until rhubarb softens and pudding thickens and begins to boil, stirring constantly. Pour hot mixture into cooled piecrust. In a large bowl, whip egg whites with an electric mixer until soft peaks form. Add Sugar Twin, Brown Sugar Twin, and vanilla extract. Continue beating until stiff peaks form. Spread meringue mixture evenly over filling, being sure to seal completely to edges of piecrust. Bake 15 minutes or until meringue starts to turn golden brown. Place pie plate on a wire rack and allow to cool 15 minutes. Refrigerate for at least 1 hour. Cut into 8 servings.

HINTS: 1. Egg whites beat best at room temperature.

2. Meringue pie cuts easily if you dip a sharp knife in warm water before slicing.

Each serving equals:

HE: 1 Vegetable • ½ Bread • ¼ Protein • ¾ Slider • 15 Optional Calories

155 Calories • 7 gm Fat • 2 gm Protein • 21 gm Carbohydrate • 238 mg Sodium • 53 mg Calcium • 1 gm Fiber

DIABETIC: 1½ Starch/Carbohydrate • 1 Fat

"Custard" Strawberry Pie

My grandma used to make delectable custard pies of all varieties, but making that exquisite custard took time, and a lot of sugar, eggs, and cream. Here's my version of a beloved favorite made with untraditional ingredients, but still spectacularly smooth and oh-so-creamy!

◐ Serves 8

1 Pillsbury refrigerated unbaked 9-inch piecrust

2 cups sliced fresh strawberries

1 (4-serving) package JELL-O sugar-free vanilla cook-and-serve pudding mix

⅔ cup Carnation Nonfat Dry Milk Powder

2 cups water

1 teaspoon vanilla extract

Preheat oven to 450 degrees. Place piecrust in a 9-inch pie plate. Flute edges and prick bottom and sides with the tines of a fork. Bake for 9 to 11 minutes or until lightly browned. Place pie plate on a wire rack and allow to cool completely. Evenly arrange strawberries in cooled crust. In a medium saucepan, combine dry pudding mix, dry milk powder, and water. Cook over medium heat until mixture thickens and starts to boil, stirring constantly. Remove from heat. Stir in vanilla extract. Pour hot pudding mixture over strawberries. Place pie plate on a wire rack and allow to cool for 15 minutes. Refrigerate for at least 2 hours. Cut into 8 servings.

HINT: Good topped with 1 tablespoon Cool Whip Lite, but don't forget to count the few additional calories.

Each serving equals:

HE: ½ Bread • ¼ Fruit • ¼ Skim Milk • ¾ Slider

163 Calories • 7 gm Fat • 3 gm Protein •
22 gm Carbohydrate • 296 mg Sodium •
74 mg Calcium • 0 gm Fiber

DIABETIC: 1½ Starch/Carbohydrate • 1 Fat

Cranberry-Apple Walnut Pie ❄

Cranberry season isn't all that long, but it's the best time to make this old-fashioned dessert that doubles up the cranberry goodness by using both berries and juice! The delectable aromas that fill your kitchen will draw hungry family members from all over the house!

◑ Serves 8

> 1 Pillsbury refrigerated unbaked 9-inch piecrust
> ½ cup Sugar Twin or Sprinkle Sweet
> ¼ cup Brown Sugar Twin
> 6 tablespoons all-purpose flour
> 1 teaspoon ground cinnamon
> 3 cups (6 small) peeled, cored, and diced cooking apples
> 1½ cups cranberries, coarsely chopped
> ¼ cup (1 ounce) chopped walnuts
> ½ cup reduced-calorie cranberry juice cocktail
> ½ cup Cool Whip Lite

Preheat oven to 425 degrees. Place piecrust in a 9-inch pie plate and flute edges. In a large bowl, combine Sugar Twin, Brown Sugar Twin, flour, and cinnamon. Add apples, cranberries, and walnuts. Mix well to combine. Stir in cranberry juice cocktail. Spread mixture evenly into piecrust. Bake for 40 minutes. Place pie plate on a wire rack and allow to cool. Cut into 8 servings. When serving, top each piece with 1 tablespoon Cool Whip Lite.

Each serving equals:

HE: 1 Fruit • ¾ Bread • ¼ Fat • ¾ Slider •
16 Optional Calories

213 Calories • 9 gm Fat • 2 gm Protein •
31 gm Carbohydrate • 101 mg Sodium •
13 mg Calcium • 2 gm Fiber

DIABETIC: 1 Fruit • 1 Starch • 1 Fat

Fresh Blueberry Pie

When the blueberries are so ripe they almost split open when you touch them, quick—stir them (gently!) into this pie that celebrates the unforgettable flavors of summer! Does working with a piecrust make you nervous? Don't succumb, just stay calm and I know you can do it!

◐ Serves 8

> 1 Pillsbury refrigerated unbaked 9-inch piecrust
> 1 (4-serving) package JELL-O sugar-free vanilla cook-and-serve pudding mix
> 1 (4-serving) package JELL-O sugar-free lemon gelatin
> 1⅓ cups water
> 1½ cups fresh blueberries

Let piecrust set at room temperature for 10 minutes. Meanwhile, in a medium saucepan, combine dry pudding mix, dry gelatin, and water. Cook over medium heat until mixture starts to boil, stirring often. Remove from heat. Stir in blueberries. Place saucepan on a wire rack and let set for 5 minutes. Cut the piecrust in half on the folded line. Gently roll each half into a ball. Wipe counter with a wet cloth and place a sheet of waxed paper over damp spot. Place one of the balls on the waxed paper. Cover with another piece of waxed paper and roll out into a 9-inch circle, with rolling pin. Carefully remove waxed paper from one side and place crust into an 8-inch pie plate. Remove other piece of waxed paper. Evenly spoon blueberry mixture into piecrust. Repeat process of rolling out remaining piecrust half. Place second crust over top of pie and flute edges. Make about 8 slashes with a knife to allow steam to escape. Bake at 450 degrees for 10 minutes. Reduce heat to 350 degrees and continue baking for 40 to 45 minutes. Place pie plate on a wire rack and allow to cool completely. Cut into 8 servings.

HINTS: 1. Place piece of uncooked elbow macaroni upright in center of pie to keep filling from cooking out of crust.

2. Frozen, well-drained blueberries may be used in place of fresh.

Each serving equals:

HE: ½ Bread • ¼ Fruit • ¾ Slider •
5 Optional Calories

147 Calories • 7 gm Fat • 1 gm Protein •
20 gm Carbohydrate • 294 mg Sodium •
2 mg Calcium • 1 gm Fiber

DIABETIC: 1 Starch • Carbohydrate • 1 Fat

Impossible Cheesecake with Fruit Glaze

It just doesn't seem possible that any low-fat, low-sugar cheesecake could taste this great—but it's true! When you bring this dessert to the table, the gorgeously glazed top will evoke oohs and aahs from family and friends. Just smile and nod when they say, "Oh, you must have slaved for hours to make this!" ☻ Serves 8

2 (8-ounce) packages Philadelphia fat-free cream cheese

⅔ cup Carnation Nonfat Dry Milk Powder

1 (4-serving) package JELL-O sugar-free instant vanilla pudding mix

¾ cup Bisquick Reduced Fat Baking Mix

2 eggs or equivalent in egg substitute

½ teaspoon vanilla extract

1 cup water

½ cup strawberry spreadable fruit

½ cup Cool Whip Lite

Preheat oven to 350 degrees. Spray a 9-inch pie plate with butter-flavored cooking spray. In a large bowl, stir cream cheese with a spoon until soft. Add dry milk powder, dry pudding mix, baking mix, eggs, vanilla, and water. Mix well using a wire whisk. Pour batter into prepared pie plate. Bake for 40 to 45 minutes or until center is firm. Evenly spread spreadable fruit over warm cheesecake. Place pie plate on a wire rack and allow to cool completely. Cut into 8 servings. When serving, top each piece with 1 tablespoon Cool Whip Lite.

HINTS: 1. Spreadable fruit spreads best at room temperature.
2. Substitute any flavor spreadable fruit.

Each serving equals:

HE: 1¼ Protein (¼ limited) • 1 Fruit • ½ Bread • ¼ Skim Milk • ¼ Slider • 3 Optional Calories

183 Calories • 3 gm Fat • 12 gm Protein • 27 gm Carbohydrate • 682 mg Sodium • 84 mg Calcium • 0 gm Fiber

DIABETIC: 1 Starch/Carbohydrate • 1 Fruit • 1 Meat

Moist Apple Caramel Cake ❄

Love and marriage, horse and carriage, apples and caramel—all perfect matches! This delectable cake is so luscious and so much like the cakes Grandma used to bake, you'll practically swoon with the sweet memories! Yum, yum, yum!   ◑   Serves 8

1½ cups Bisquick Reduced Fat Baking Mix
1 (4-serving) package JELL-O sugar-free instant vanilla pudding mix
1 cup unsweetened apple juice
2 tablespoons water
¼ cup (1 ounce) chopped walnuts
1 cup (2 small) unpeeled, cored, and chopped cooking apples
2 tablespoons caramel sauce

Preheat oven to 350 degrees. Spray a 9-by-9-inch cake pan with butter-flavored cooking spray. In a large bowl, combine baking mix and dry pudding mix. Add apple juice, water, walnuts, and apples. Mix gently to combine. Spread batter into prepared cake pan. Drizzle caramel sauce evenly over top. Bake for 40 to 50 minutes or until a toothpick inserted in center comes out clean. Place cake pan on a wire rack and allow to cool completely. Cut into 8 servings.

HINTS: 1. Good topped with 1 tablespoon Cool Whip Lite, but don't forget to count the few additional calories.

2. This will be a moist, heavy cake.

Each serving equals:

HE: 1 Bread • ½ Fruit • ¼ Fat • ¼ Slider •
4 Optional Calories

160 Calories • 4 gm Fat • 2 gm Protein •
29 gm Carbohydrate • 446 mg Sodium •
28 mg Calcium • 1 gm Fiber

DIABETIC: 1 Fruit • 1 Starch/Carbohydrate *or*
2 Starch/Carbohydrate

Angel Loaf Cake

Don't turn your back on this light and lovely classic cake, or it might just fly away! This cake is extra-special when served with some fresh berries or a dab of Cool Whip Lite, so try as many different possibilities as you can imagine! ☻ Serves 12

1 cup cake flour
1½ cups Sugar Twin or Sprinkle Sweet ☆
12 egg whites
1½ teaspoons cream of tartar
1 tablespoon vanilla extract
¼ teaspoon salt

Preheat oven to 350 degrees. In a small bowl, combine cake flour and ¾ cup Sugar Twin. Mix well using a wire whisk. Place egg whites in a very large mixing bowl. Beat egg whites with an electric mixer on HIGH until foamy. Add cream of tartar, vanilla extract, and salt. Continue beating until stiff enough to form soft peaks. Add remaining ¾ cup Sugar Twin, 2 tablespoons at a time, while continuing to beat egg whites until stiff peaks form. Add the flour mixture, ½ cup at a time, folding in with spatula or wire whisk. Pour batter into an *ungreased* 9-by-13-inch metal cake pan. Bake for 25 to 30 minutes or until cake springs back when lightly touched. DO NOT OVERBAKE. Place cake pan on a wire rack and allow to cool. Cut into 12 servings.

HINTS: 1. Egg whites beat best at room temperature.

2. Cover leftovers to prevent drying.

Each serving equals:

HE: ⅓ Bread • ⅓ Protein • ¼ Slider •
1 Optional Calorie

56 Calories • 0 gm Fat • 5 gm Protein •
9 gm Carbohydrate • 100 mg Sodium •
4 mg Calcium • 0 gm Fiber

DIABETIC: ½ Starch/Carbohydrate

Pecan Tassies

Remember how they say that good things come in small packages? These miniature pies prove it's oh-so-deliciously-true! You get not one but two in a serving, so you can double your pleasure and double your fun when you serve these pecan treats!

● Serves 8 (2 each)

> 1 Pillsbury refrigerated unbaked 9-inch piecrust
> 1 (4-serving) package JELL-O sugar-free vanilla cook-and-serve pudding mix
> 2 tablespoons Brown Sugar Twin
> 1¼ cups water
> 1 teaspoon vanilla extract
> ¼ cup (1 ounce) chopped pecans
> 2 tablespoons quick oats

Preheat oven to 400 degrees. Unfold piecrust. Using a 2½-inch biscuit cutter, cut 12 circles. Press dough scraps together and cut out 4 more circles, for a total of 16 circles. Place pastry circles into 16 miniature muffin cups. Press to form tarts. In a medium saucepan, combine dry pudding mix, Brown Sugar Twin, and water. Stir in vanilla extract, pecans, and oats. Cook over medium heat until mixture thickens and starts to boil, stirring constantly. Evenly spoon about 1 teaspoon mixture into each crust. Bake for 18 to 22 minutes. Place muffin pans on a wire rack and allow to cool for 10 minutes. Remove from pans and continue cooling. Refrigerate leftovers.

Each serving equals:

HE: ½ Bread • ½ Fat • ¾ Slider • 6 Optional Calories

157 Calories • 9 gm Fat • 1 gm Protein •
18 gm Carbohydrate • 158 mg Sodium • 2 mg Calcium •
1 gm Fiber

DIABETIC: 1½ Fat • 1 Starch/Carbohydrate

Banana Split Dessert Pizza

Creating scrumptious new "banana split" desserts is an annual occasion with me—I come up with at least a couple of new ones every year! These man-pleasing and kid-pleasing favorites are almost as much fun to prepare as they are to eat. When you're planning a birthday or anniversary party and you want a show-stopping presentation, look no further than this dazzler!   ●   Serves 12

1 (8-serving) package Pillsbury Reduced Fat Crescent Rolls

1 (8-ounce) package Philadelphia fat-free cream cheese

2 teaspoons coconut extract ☆

¼ cup Sugar Twin or Sprinkle Sweet ☆

2 cups (2 medium) finely chopped bananas

1 cup finely chopped fresh strawberries

2 (4-serving) packages JELL-O sugar-free instant banana pudding
    mix

1⅔ cups Carnation Nonfat Dry Milk Powder ☆

2 cups (two 8-ounce cans) crushed pineapple, packed in fruit juice,
    undrained

1 cup water

¾ cup Yoplait plain fat-free yogurt

1½ cups Cool Whip Free

3 tablespoons (¾ ounce) chopped pecans

3 tablespoons flaked coconut

2 tablespoons (½ ounce) mini chocolate chips

3 maraschino cherries, cut into 4 pieces

Preheat oven to 425 degrees. Pat rolls into an ungreased 10-by-15-inch rimmed baking sheet. Gently press dough to cover bottom of pan, being sure to seal perforations. Bake for 6 to 8 minutes or until golden brown. Place baking sheet on a wire rack and allow to cool. In a small bowl, stir cream cheese with a spoon until soft. Stir in 1 teaspoon coconut extract and 2 tablespoons Sugar Twin. Spread mixture evenly over cooled crust. Evenly sprinkle bananas and strawberries over cream cheese mixture. In a medium bowl, combine dry pudding mixes and 1⅓ cups dry milk powder. Add undrained pineapple and water. Mix well using a wire whisk. Spread pudding mixture evenly over bananas. Refrigerate for at least 30 minutes. In a medium bowl, combine yogurt and remaining ⅓ cup dry milk powder. Add remaining 1 teaspoon coconut extract and remaining 2 tablespoons Sugar Twin. Blend in Cool Whip Free. Spread topping mixture evenly over set pudding layer. Evenly sprinkle pecans, coconut, and chocolate chips over top. Garnish with maraschino cherry pieces. Refrigerate for at least 30 minutes. Cut into 12 servings.

HINTS: 1. DO NOT use inexpensive rolls as they don't cover the pan properly.

2. To prevent bananas from turning brown, mix with 1 teaspoon lemon juice or sprinkle with Fruit Fresh.

Each serving equals:

HE: ¾ Fruit • ⅔ Bread • ½ Skim Milk • ⅓ Protein •
¼ Fat • ¼ Slider • 19 Optional Calories

233 Calories • 5 gm Fat • 9 gm Protein •
38 gm Carbohydrate • 565 mg Sodium •
154 mg Calcium • 1 gm Fiber

DIABETIC: 1½ Starch/Carbohydrate • 1 Fruit • ½ Fat

Majestic Raspberry-Almond Cream Torte

If you ever dreamed of being an architect but never got to build anything big, why not start with this recipe? You'll feel like the creator of an edible skyscraper when you layer one scrumptious flavor on top of another! ☻ Serves 4

½ cup raspberry spreadable fruit
¾ cup Cool Whip Free
½ teaspoon almond extract
6 (2½-inch x 5-inch) chocolate graham crackers
1 tablespoon (¼ ounce) chopped almonds
1 tablespoon (¼ ounce) mini chocolate chips

In a medium bowl, stir spreadable fruit until softened. Stir in Cool Whip Free and almond extract. Mix well to combine. Cover and refrigerate mixture for 10 minutes. On a flat dessert serving plate, arrange 1 graham cracker. Spread 2 tablespoons of topping mixture over cracker. Layer with another cracker and another 2 tablespoons topping. Continue layering until all crackers are used. Frost top and sides with remaining topping. Evenly sprinkle almonds and chocolate chips over top. Cover and refrigerate for at least 1 hour. Slice into 4 pieces.

Each serving equals:

HE: 2 Fruit • ½ Bread • ½ Slider •
1 Optional Calorie

162 Calories • 2 gm Fat • 1 gm Protein •
35 gm Carbohydrate • 75 mg Sodium •
5 mg Calcium • 1 gm Fiber

DIABETIC: 2 Fruit • 1 Starch/Carbohydrate

Lemon Bars

Mayonnaise in cookies? Yogurt, okay, and sour cream, of course, but mayo in a lemon cookie? Trust me, this works so well, you'll feel like a culinary genius. These look lovely and taste just wonderful, so try serving them at an afternoon tea or for a card party with friends.

○ Serves 8 (2 each)

> 1½ cups Bisquick Reduced Fat Baking Mix
> 2 (4-serving) packages JELL-O sugar-free lemon gelatin
> ⅓ cup Yoplait plain fat-free yogurt
> ¼ cup Kraft fat-free mayonnaise
> ½ cup Land O Lakes no-fat sour cream
> 2 teaspoons powdered sugar, optional

Preheat oven to 350 degrees. Spray a 9-by-13-inch cake pan with butter-flavored cooking spray. In a large bowl, combine baking mix and dry gelatin. Add yogurt, mayonnaise, and sour cream. Mix well to combine. Spread batter into prepared cake pan. Bake for 20 to 25 minutes. Sprinkle top with powdered sugar. Place cake pan on a wire rack and allow to cool completely. Cut into 16 bars.

Each serving equals:

HE: 1 Bread • ¼ Slider • 9 Optional Calories

109 Calories • 1 gm Fat • 4 gm Protein •
21 gm Carbohydrate • 408 mg Sodium • 53 mg Calcium •
0 gm Fiber

DIABETIC: 1½ Starch/Carbohydrate

Apple Brown Betty

Here's another "comfort food" recipe no self-respecting grandma-in-training can afford to be without! This is surprisingly easy to fix, smells yummy while it's baking, and serves up so crumbly and tasty, no one would dare say no to dessert!   ☻   Serves 4

> 2 cups (4 small) peeled and sliced cooking apples
>
> 1 tablespoon lemon juice
>
> 3 tablespoons Sugar Twin or Sprinkle Sweet
>
> 1 teaspoon ground cinnamon
>
> 12 (2½-inch) graham cracker squares, made into crumbs
>
> 1 tablespoon + 1 teaspoon reduced-calorie margarine, melted
>
> ¾ cup hot water

Preheat oven to 350 degrees. Spray an 8-by-8-inch baking dish with butter-flavored cooking spray. Evenly arrange apples in prepared baking dish. Sprinkle lemon juice, Sugar Twin, and cinnamon evenly over top. Toss well to combine. In a small bowl, combine graham cracker crumbs and melted margarine. Sprinkle crumb mixture evenly over apple mixture. Pour hot water evenly over top. Cover and bake for 30 minutes. Uncover and continue baking for 5 to 10 minutes or until apples are tender. Divide into 4 servings. Serve warm.

> HINTS 1. A self-seal sandwich bag works great for crushing graham crackers.
>
> 2. Good served with sugar and fat-free vanilla ice cream, but don't forget to count the few additional calories.

Each serving equals:

HE: 1 Fruit • 1 Bread • ½ Fat • 5 Optional Calories

90 Calories • 2 gm Fat • 1 gm Protein •
17 gm Carbohydrate • 87 mg Sodium • 11 mg Calcium •
2 gm Fiber

DIABETIC: 1 Fruit • ½ Fat

Walnut Brownies

Pudding provides a terrific touch in this recipe, as does the applesauce. For moist and nutty brownies too good to be good-for-you, stir up a batch of these next time you're feeding the Cub Scouts or even (I know!) your daughter's Brownie troop.   ❂   Serves 8 (2 each)

> 1 cup all-purpose flour
> 1 (4-serving) package JELL-O sugar-free instant chocolate fudge pudding mix
> ¼ cup Sugar Twin or Sprinkle Sweet
> 1 teaspoon baking powder
> 1 cup unsweetened applesauce
> 1 egg or equivalent in egg substitute
> 1 teaspoon vanilla extract
> ¼ cup (1 ounce) chopped walnuts

Preheat oven to 325 degrees. Spray an 8-by-8-inch baking dish with butter-flavored cooking spray. In a medium bowl, combine flour, dry pudding mix, Sugar Twin, and baking powder. In a small bowl, combine applesauce, egg, and vanilla extract. Add applesauce mixture to flour mixture. Mix well until mixture is smooth. Stir in walnuts. Spread batter into prepared baking dish. Bake for 20 to 25 minutes. Place baking dish on a wire rack and allow to cool. Cut into 16 squares.

Each serving equals:

HE: ⅔ Bread • ½ Fruit • ¼ Fat • ¼ Protein • ¼ Slider • 1 Optional Calorie

119 Calories • 3 gm Fat • 3 gm Protein • 20 gm Carbohydrate • 235 mg Sodium • 44 mg Calcium • 1 gm Fiber

DIABETIC: 1 Starch/Carbohydrate • ½ Fat

Mince Tarts

It just doesn't seem like the holidays without a mince dessert, does it? Now you and your family can enjoy this super-easy method for making mini "mince pies"! Just take one bite, and you'll shout, "Joy to the world!"   ♥   Serves 6

> 1 (4-serving) package JELL-O sugar-free vanilla cook-and-serve pudding mix
> 1 teaspoon apple pie spice
> 1 cup water
> 6 tablespoons raisins
> 1½ cups (3 small) cored, peeled, and finely diced cooking apples
> ½ teaspoon rum extract
> 1 (6-single serve) package Keebler graham cracker crusts
> 6 tablespoons Cool Whip Lite

In a medium saucepan, combine dry pudding mix, apple pie spice, and water. Add raisins and apples. Mix well to combine. Cook over medium heat until mixture thickens and apples start to soften, stirring often. Remove from heat. Stir in rum extract. Evenly spoon hot mixture into graham cracker crusts. Refrigerate for at least 30 minutes. When serving, top each with 1 tablespoon Cool Whip Lite.

Each serving equals:

HE: 1 Fruit • ½ Bread • ¾ Slider •
3 Optional Calories

191 Calories • 7 gm Fat • 1 gm Protein •
31 gm Carbohydrate • 371 mg Sodium •
6 mg Calcium • 1 gm Fiber

DIABETIC: 1 Fruit • 1 Starch • 1 Fat

This and That

Just as you enjoyed digging through Grandma's "junk" drawer or burrowing through the attic to find long-lost treasures, I hope you'll savor a journey through this section of recipes. They don't fit anywhere else, but they definitely shouldn't be missed! Here's where a game of hide-and-seek through Grandma's recipe box turns up delectable muffins and homemade coffee cakes, plus those yummy accompaniments she served to make every meal perfect.

You can bring the family together for brunch when you put Spanish Breakfast Bake on the menu; you will surely dazzle your kids with my Peanut Butter Popcorn Balls; and whether you're whipping up a speedy corn relish for a late-summer picnic or a quick bread sure to become a new holiday tradition, you've made Grandma's Comfort Food your own!

This and That

Breakfast Casserole

This is a great solution for breakfast for a crowd, so that you're not stuck at the stove frying up eggs for everyone. By stirring up one or two of these rich casseroles, you'll be able to enjoy sitting with your company instead of feeling like Cinderella in the kitchen.

Serves 6

6 slices reduced-calorie white bread, diced
1 full cup (6 ounces) diced Dubuque 97% fat-free ham or any extra-lean ham
½ cup (one 2.5-ounce jar) sliced mushrooms, drained
¼ cup diced onion
¼ cup diced green bell pepper
¾ cup (3 ounces) shredded Kraft reduced-fat Cheddar cheese
4 eggs or equivalent in egg substitute
1½ cups (one 12-fluid-ounce can) Carnation Evaporated Skim Milk
¼ teaspoon lemon pepper

Spray an 8-by-8-inch baking dish with butter-flavored cooking spray. Place half of diced bread on bottom of dish. Layer ham, mushrooms, onion, green pepper, and cheese over bread. Place remaining bread on top. In a medium bowl, beat eggs with a wire whisk. Add evaporated skim milk and lemon pepper. Mix well to combine. Pour egg mixture over bread. Cover and refrigerate overnight. Bake for 45 minutes at 350 degrees. Uncover and bake an additional 10 minutes. Place baking dish on a wire rack and let set for 10 minutes. Divide into 6 servings.

Each serving equals:

HE: 2 Protein (⅔ limited) • ½ Bread • ½ Skim Milk •
⅓ Vegetable

219 Calories • 7 gm Fat • 20 gm Protein •
19 gm Carbohydrate • 645 mg Sodium •
315 mg Calcium • 3 gm Fiber

DIABETIC: 2 Meat • 1 Starch/Carbohydrate

Spanish Breakfast Bake

Here's another terrific brunch idea that lets the oven do the cooking, so you can do the visiting, whether you've got a houseful of guests or it's just your family gathered around the table. The aroma from this spicy meat-and-potatoes dish will get even the laziest child up and out of bed! ☻ Serves 6

8 ounces ground 90% lean turkey or beef

½ teaspoon poultry seasoning

¼ teaspoon ground sage

¼ teaspoon garlic powder

3 cups (10 ounces) shredded loose-packed frozen potatoes

4 eggs, beaten, or equivalent in egg substitute

⅔ cup Carnation Nonfat Dry Milk Powder

¾ cup water

¾ cup chunky salsa (mild, medium, or hot)

⅓ cup (1½ ounces) shredded Kraft reduced-fat Cheddar cheese

Preheat oven to 350 degrees. Spray an 8-by-8-inch baking dish with butter-flavored cooking spray. In a large skillet sprayed with butter-flavored cooking spray, brown meat. Stir in poultry seasoning, sage, and garlic powder. Layer potatoes in prepared baking dish. Place browned meat mixture over potatoes. In a medium bowl, combine eggs, dry milk powder, and water. Add salsa. Mix well to combine. Pour egg mixture evenly over potato mixture. Bake for 1 hour or until eggs are almost set. Sprinkle Cheddar cheese over top and bake an additional 10 minutes. Place baking dish on a wire rack and let set for 5 to 10 minutes. Divide into 6 servings. If desired, garnish with additional salsa and fat-free sour cream.

HINT: Mr. Dell's frozen shredded potatoes are a good choice or raw shredded potatoes may be used in place of frozen potatoes.

Each serving equals:

HE: 2 Protein (⅔ limited) • ⅓ Bread • ⅓ Skim Milk •
¼ Vegetable

188 Calories • 8 gm Fat • 16 gm Protein •
13 gm Carbohydrate • 288 mg Sodium •
197 mg Calcium • 1 gm Fiber

DIABETIC: 2 Meat • 1 Starch/Carbohydrate •
½ Vegetable

Garden Salsa

If you've got a garden full of ripe tomatoes or you've just bought out the local farm stand because all those fresh veggies looked so good, why not chop, chop, chop—and make jars of your own fresh salsa? This easy recipe lets you choose whether to go hot-hot-hot or not-not-not, and also lets you make as much or as little as you like.

☻ Makes 8 cups

> 6 cups peeled and chopped fresh tomatoes
> 1 cup chopped onion
> 1 cup chopped green bell pepper
> ¼ cup lemon juice
> ¼ cup fresh parsley
> 1 teaspoon dried minced garlic
> ¼ teaspoon black pepper
> 1 cup (one 8-ounce can) Hunt's Tomato Sauce

In a large glass bowl, combine tomatoes, onion, and green pepper. Place 1½ cups of tomato mixture in a blender container. Add lemon juice, parsley, garlic, black pepper, and tomato sauce. Cover and process on BLEND for 20 seconds or until mixture is pureed. Pour blended mixture into bowl with remaining tomato mixture. Mix well to combine. Cover and refrigerate at least 2 hours.

HINTS: 1. Recipe can be cut in half.

2. Canned green chili peppers may be added.

Each one-tablespoon serving equals:

HE: 4 Optional Calories

4 Calories • 0 gm Fat • 0 gm Protein •
1 gm Carbohydrate • 13 mg Sodium •
1 mg Calcium • 0 gm Fiber

DIABETIC: Free Vegetable

Old Time Corn Relish

Corn relish is a delightful Iowa tradition I'd like to share with you, especially since this homemade version is so much tastier than the kind you buy in a jar. What's also nice is that you can make it fresh whenever you're in the mood to serve it.

◐ Serves 6 (⅓ cup)

> 2 cups (one 16-ounce can) cream-style corn
> ½ cup pickle relish
> 1 tablespoon white vinegar
> 1 teaspoon dried onion flakes
> 2 tablespoons Sugar Twin

In a medium bowl, combine corn, pickle relish, vinegar, onion flakes, and Sugar Twin. Mix well to combine. Cover and refrigerate for at least 30 minutes.

Each serving equals:

HE: ⅔ Bread • ¼ Slider • 2 Optional Calories

92 Calories • 0 gm Fat • 1 gm Protein • 22 gm Carbohydrate • 389 mg Sodium • 7 mg Calcium • 1 gm Fiber

DIABETIC: 1 Starch

Private Label Grape Jelly

Did you ever think you'd be making homemade jelly? Even if your mother or grandmother taught you how, it takes a lot of time—and a lot of fruit! Except when you do it the Healthy Exchanges "grandma" way . . . and please young and old alike.

○ Makes about 3 cups

> 3 cups unsweetened grape juice
> ¼ cup Quick Cooking Minute Tapioca
> ¼ cup Sugar Twin or Sprinkle Sweet
> 1 (4-serving) package JELL-O sugar-free cherry gelatin

Pour grape juice into a medium saucepan. Cook over medium heat until juice starts to boil. Add tapioca and continue cooking until slightly thickened and tapioca is clear. Remove from heat. Stir in Sugar Twin and dry gelatin. Mix well to dissolve gelatin. Pour into jars. Cool completely. Cover and refrigerate for at least 24 hours. Will keep for 2 weeks in refrigerator.

Each one-tablespoon serving equals:

HE: 12 Optional Calories

12 Calories • 0 gm Fat • 0 gm Protein • 3 gm Carbohydrate • 5 mg Sodium • 1 mg Calcium • 0 gm Fiber

DIABETIC: 1 Free Food

Grilled Peanut Butter and Jelly Sandwiches

I always believe in making what's good better, and this recipe is a perfect example. Peanut butter and jelly is a classic, and your kids could eat it every time, couldn't they? But watch their faces when you bring these sandwiches to the table—and share their delight!

☻ Serves 4

¼ cup grape spreadable fruit
8 slices reduced-calorie bread
¼ cup Peter Pan reduced-fat peanut butter

Spread 1 tablespoon spreadable fruit on 4 slices of bread. Spread 1 tablespoon peanut butter on remaining 4 slices. For each sandwich, place 2 slices together. Spray a griddle or large skillet with butter-flavored cooking spray. Grill sandwiches for 3 to 4 minutes on each side or until golden brown. Serve at once.

Each serving equals:

HE: 1 Bread • 1 Fruit • 1 Fat • 1 Protein

218 Calories • 6 gm Fat • 9 gm Protein •
32 gm Carbohydrate • 305 mg Sodium •
35 mg Calcium • 6 gm Fiber

DIABETIC: 1½ Starch/Carbohydrate • 1 Fruit • 1 Fat •
½ Meat

Cranberry-Orange Sauce

Here's a luscious fruity sauce to ladle over fat-free and sugar-free ice cream, or to pour over pancakes or French toast. This particular combination of flavors is so wonderful, there's even a sorbet that features them! ☻ Serves 6 (½ cup)

> 1 (4-serving) package JELL-O sugar-free orange gelatin
> 1 (4-serving) package JELL-O sugar-free vanilla cook-and-serve pudding mix
> 1¾ cups water
> 2 cups fresh or frozen cranberries

In a large saucepan, combine dry gelatin, dry pudding mix, and water. Stir in cranberries. Cook over medium heat for 10 to 12 minutes or until cranberries become soft, stirring often. Place pan on a wire rack and let set 5 minutes. Pour mixture into a covered container and refrigerate for at least 1 hour. Gently stir again just before serving.

Each serving equals:

HE: ⅓ Fruit • ¼ Slider

36 Calories • 0 gm Fat • 1 gm Protein •
8 gm Carbohydrate • 113 mg Sodium • 3 mg Calcium •
1 gm Fiber

DIABETIC: 1 Fruit

Ham and Cheddar Spread

If you're looking for something heartier than onion dip to serve at a cocktail party, this is a great combination! It's tangy, it's intensely flavorful—and you can serve it in lots of ways.

☻ Serves 4 (full ¼ cup)

> 1 (8-ounce) package Philadelphia fat-free cream cheese
>
> 2 teaspoons prepared mustard
>
> 1 teaspoon dried onion flakes
>
> 1 teaspoon dried parsley flakes
>
> ⅓ cup (1½ ounces) shredded Kraft reduced-fat Cheddar cheese
>
> ½ cup (3 ounces) finely diced Dubuque 97% fat-free ham or any
> extra-lean ham

In a medium bowl, stir cream cheese with a spoon until soft. Add mustard, onion flakes, and parsley flakes. Mix well to combine. Stir in Cheddar cheese and ham. Cover and refrigerate for at least 30 minutes. Good on celery, bread, or crackers.

Each serving equals:

HE: 2 Protein

95 Calories • 3 gm Fat • 14 gm Protein •
3 gm Carbohydrate • 639 mg Sodium • 72 mg Calcium •
0 gm Fiber

DIABETIC: 2 Meat

Harvest Time Zucchini-Carrot Muffins

These have the most amazing golden color when they emerge from the oven—not to mention an irresistible aroma! Serve these in a pretty basket lined with a cloth napkin, and show your family that anytime they're seated together around your table is a special occasion!

☻ Serves 8

1½ cups all-purpose flour
½ cup Sugar Twin or Sprinkle Sweet
2 teaspoons baking powder
½ cup grated carrots
½ cup grated unpeeled zucchini
½ cup raisins
2 eggs, beaten, or equivalent in egg substitute
2 tablespoons vegetable oil
2 teaspoons vanilla extract
¼ cup skim milk

Preheat oven to 375 degrees. Spray 8 wells of a 12-hole muffin pan with butter-flavored cooking spray or line with paper liners. In a large bowl, combine flour, Sugar Twin, and baking powder. Blend in carrots, zucchini, and raisins. In a small bowl, combine eggs, vegetable oil, vanilla extract, and skim milk. Add egg mixture to flour mixture. Mix gently just to combine. Evenly spoon batter into prepared muffin wells. Bake for 20 to 22 minutes or until a toothpick inserted in center comes out clean. Place muffin pan on a wire rack and let set for 5 minutes. Remove muffins from pan and continue cooling on wire rack.

HINT: Fill unused muffin wells with water. It protects the muffin tin and ensures even baking.

Each serving equals:

HE: 1 Bread • ¾ Fat • ½ Fruit • ¼ Vegetable •
¼ Protein (limited) • 9 Optional Calories

165 Calories • 5 gm Fat • 5 gm Protein •
25 gm Carbohydrate • 146 mg Sodium •
93 mg Calcium • 1 gm Fiber

DIABETIC: 1½ Starch/Carbohydrate • 1 Fat

Vanilla–Poppy Seed Muffins ❄

If you've never baked with poppy seeds before, you'll be pleasantly surprised to discover what a delectable flavor they have, especially when combined with vanilla! The yogurt keeps these muffins moist and adds a nice dollop of calcium. ☺ Serves 8

1½ cups Bisquick Reduced Fat Baking Mix
1 (4-serving) package JELL-O sugar-free instant vanilla pudding mix
⅓ cup Carnation Nonfat Dry Milk Powder
1 tablespoon poppy seeds
¾ cup Yoplait plain fat-free yogurt
¼ cup water
1 egg, beaten, or equivalent in egg substitute
2 teaspoons vanilla extract

Preheat oven to 400 degrees. Spray 8 wells of a 12-hole muffin pan with butter-flavored cooking spray or line with paper liners. In a large bowl, combine baking mix, dry pudding mix, dry milk powder, and poppy seeds. In a small bowl, combine yogurt, water, egg, and vanilla extract. Add yogurt mixture to baking mix mixture. Mix just until combined. Evenly fill prepared muffin wells. Bake for 15 to 20 minutes or until a toothpick inserted in center comes out clean. Place muffin pan on a wire rack and let set for 5 minutes. Remove muffins from pan and continue cooling on wire rack.

HINT: Fill unused muffin wells with water. It protects the muffin tin and ensures even baking.

Each serving equals:

HE: 1 Bread • ¼ Skim Milk • ¼ Slider •
2 Optional Calories

126 Calories • 2 gm Fat • 5 gm Protein •
22 gm Carbohydrate • 466 mg Sodium •
98 mg Calcium • 0 gm Fiber

DIABETIC: 1½ Starch/Carbohydrate

Festive Holiday Bread

Quick breads are great to give as gifts, and they're also perfect for serving to unexpected guests and visiting Christmas carolers. This one overflows with all kinds of goodies, so nibbling on a slice is like opening a gift!

● Serves 8 (1 thick or 2 thin slices)

$1\frac{1}{2}$ cups all-purpose flour
1 (4-serving) package JELL-O sugar-free instant vanilla pudding mix
$\frac{1}{3}$ cup Sugar Twin or Sprinkle Sweet
1 teaspoon baking soda
$\frac{1}{2}$ teaspoon baking powder
$\frac{1}{2}$ cup Land O Lakes no-fat sour cream
$\frac{1}{4}$ cup skim milk
1 egg or equivalent in egg substitute
$\frac{2}{3}$ cup (2 medium) mashed ripe banana
8 maraschino cherries, quartered
$\frac{1}{4}$ cup (1 ounce) chopped walnuts
2 tablespoons ($\frac{1}{2}$ ounce) mini chocolate chips

Preheat oven to 350 degrees. Spray a 9-by-5-inch loaf pan with butter-flavored cooking spray. In a large bowl, combine flour, dry pudding mix, Sugar Twin, baking soda, and baking powder. In a medium bowl, combine sour cream and skim milk. Add egg. Mix well to combine. Stir in mashed banana. Add sour cream mixture to flour mixture. Mix gently just to combine. Gently stir in cherries, walnuts, and chocolate chips. Spread mixture into prepared loaf pan. Bake for 45 to 50 minutes or until a toothpick inserted in center comes out clean. Place loaf pan on a wire rack and let set for 10 minutes. Remove bread from pan and continue cooling on wire rack. Cut into 8 thick or 16 thin slices.

Each serving equals:

HE: 1 Bread • $\frac{1}{2}$ Fruit • $\frac{1}{4}$ Protein • $\frac{1}{4}$ Fat • $\frac{1}{2}$ Slider • 14 Optional Calories

188 Calories • 4 gm Fat • 5 gm Protein • 33 gm Carbohydrate • 416 mg Sodium • 71 mg Calcium • 1 gm Fiber

DIABETIC: $1\frac{1}{2}$ Starch/Carbohydrate • $\frac{1}{2}$ Fruit • $\frac{1}{2}$ Fat

Blueberry Banana Coffee Cake ❄

Some mornings in summer, you wake up and feel so energized, you can't decide what to do first. I suggest you stir up this coffee cake! The combination of blueberries and bananas is unusual but oh-so-tasty, and the almonds give it an extra-special flair. While it's baking, you can spend time admiring your garden! ☻ Serves 8

1½ cups Bisquick Reduced Fat Baking Mix

1 (4-serving) package JELL-O sugar-free instant banana cream pudding mix

⅔ cup Carnation Nonfat Dry Milk Powder

¼ cup (1 ounce) slivered almonds

⅔ cup (2 medium) mashed ripe banana

1 egg, slightly beaten, or equivalent in egg substitute

1 cup unsweetened applesauce

1 teaspoon almond extract

½ cup water

1½ cups fresh blueberries

Preheat oven to 350 degrees. Spray an 8-by-8-inch baking dish with butter-flavored cooking spray. In a large bowl, combine baking mix, dry pudding mix, and dry milk powder. Stir in almonds. In a small bowl, combine mashed banana, egg, applesauce, almond extract, and water. Add banana mixture to baking mix mixture. Mix well to combine. Gently fold in blueberries. Pour mixture into prepared baking dish. Bake for 35 minutes or until a toothpick inserted in center comes out clean. Place baking dish on a wire rack and allow to cool. Cut into 8 servings.

Each serving equals:

HE: 1 Bread • 1 Fruit • ¼ Skim Milk • ¼ Fat • ¼ Protein • 13 Optional Calories

192 Calories • 4 gm Fat • 6 gm Protein • 33 gm Carbohydrate • 471 mg Sodium • 108 mg Calcium • 2 gm Fiber

DIABETIC: 1 Starch/Carbohydrate • 1 Fruit • ½ Fat

Fruitcake

Wait, I don't want you to skip this recipe just because fruitcakes have such a bad reputation! This one is definitely different. It's as full of fruit as can be, but instead of being dry and tasteless, it's wonderfully nutty and moist. Surprise your holiday guests and prove once and for all that fruitcake is BACK!   ☻   Serves 8 (1 thick or 2 thin slices)

> 1½ cups purchased graham cracker crumbs or 24 (2½-inch) graham
>   cracker squares, made into crumbs
> 1 (4-serving) package JELL-O sugar-free instant vanilla pudding mix
> 1 teaspoon pumpkin pie spice
> 1 teaspoon baking powder
> 2 cups (one 16-ounce can) fruit cocktail, packed in fruit juice,
>   drained, and ⅓ cup liquid reserved
> 1 egg or equivalent in egg substitute
> 1 teaspoon rum extract
> ¼ cup raisins
> ¼ cup (1 ounce) chopped walnuts

Preheat oven to 350 degrees. Spray a 9-by-5-inch loaf pan with butter-flavored cooking spray. In a large bowl, combine graham cracker crumbs, dry pudding mix, pumpkin pie spice, and baking powder. Add reserved fruit cocktail juice, egg, and rum extract. Mix gently to combine. Blend in fruit cocktail, raisins, and walnuts. Pour batter into prepared loaf pan. Bake for 45 to 50 minutes or until a toothpick inserted in center comes out clean. Place loaf pan on a wire rack and cool completely. Cut into 8 thick or 16 thin slices.

Each serving equals:

HE: 1 Bread • ¾ Fruit • ¼ Protein • ¼ Fat •
13 Optional Calories

---

185 Calories • 5 gm Fat • 3 gm Protein •
32 gm Carbohydrate • 373 mg Sodium •
54 mg Calcium • 2 gm Fiber

DIABETIC: 1 Fruit • 1 Starch/Carbohydrate • ½ Fat

Maple Crunch

Snacking is an important part of living healthy for the rest of your life, but it helps when you've got delicious homemade snacks to enjoy without guilt. This crunchy cereal mix is so sweet and satisfying, you'll probably have a hard time keeping the jar filled (once the family finds it!). ☻ Serves 6 (¾ cup)

⅓ cup Cary's Sugar Free Maple Syrup
1 tablespoon + 1 teaspoon reduced-calorie margarine
½ cup Sugar Twin or Sprinkle Sweet
¼ cup Brown Sugar Twin
5 cups (4½ ounces) Rice Chex

Preheat oven to 250 degrees. Spray a large cookie sheet with butter-flavored cooking spray. In a large skillet, combine maple syrup and margarine. Cook over medium heat until margarine is melted. Stir in Sugar Twin and Brown Sugar Twin. Bring mixture to a boil, then continue cooking for 2 minutes, stirring constantly. Remove from heat. Place Rice Chex on prepared cookie sheet. Drizzle syrup mixture over Rice Chex. Mix gently with a wooden spoon to coat. Bake for 60 minutes, stirring after every 15 minutes. Store in an airtight container.

Each serving equals:

HE: 1 Bread • ⅓ Fat • ¼ Slider • 1 Optional Calorie

97 Calories • 1 gm Fat • 1 gm Protein •
21 gm Carbohydrate • 217 mg Sodium • 3 mg Calcium •
0 gm Fiber

DIABETIC: 1 Starch

Peanut Butter Popcorn Balls

Here's another healthy version of a kid-pleasing favorite that I've never seen an adult say "No, thanks" to! This recipe is almost as much fun to make as it is to eat. ☻ Serves 2

1 tablespoon white corn syrup

2 tablespoons Peter Pan reduced-fat creamy peanut butter

2 tablespoons Brown Sugar Twin

½ teaspoon vanilla extract

2 cups popped popcorn

In an 8-cup glass measuring bowl, mix corn syrup, peanut butter, Brown Sugar Twin, and vanilla extract. Cover and microwave on HIGH (100% power) for 30 to 40 seconds, or until mixture begins to bubble. Stir well to combine. Add popped popcorn. Mix well to coat. Place bowl on a wire rack and let set for 2 to 3 minutes. Shape popcorn mixture into 2 balls. Cool completely. Wrap each popcorn ball in plastic wrap.

HINTS: 1. 1 tablespoon + 1 teaspoon unpopped popcorn will make about 2 cups in an air popper.

2. Balls form more easily if you dip your hands in cold water before shaping.

Each serving equals:

HE: 1 Protein • 1 Fat • ⅓ Bread • ¼ Slider • 15 Optional Calories

149 Calories • 6 gm Fat • 5 gm Protein • 21 gm Carbohydrate • 88 mg Sodium • 1 mg Calcium • 2 gm Fiber

DIABETIC: 1 Starch/Carbohydrate • ½ Meat • ½ Fat

Paradise Pineapple "Ice Cream" ❄

If you remember turning the crank of an old-fashioned ice cream freezer at Grandma's, you also remember how EXHAUSTING it could be to produce your favorite frozen treat. This version takes much less elbow grease, but the taste is sweet and smooth, as glorious as you recall! ☻ Serves 4 (1 cup)

> 1⅓ cups Carnation Nonfat Dry Milk Powder
> 3 cups water
> 2 tablespoons white vinegar
> 1 cup (one 8-ounce can) crushed pineapple, packed in fruit juice, drained
> Sugar substitute to equal ¼ cup sugar
> 1 teaspoon coconut extract

In a large bowl, combine dry milk powder, water, and vinegar. Let set 5 minutes. Stir in drained pineapple, sugar substitute, and coconut extract. Mix well using a wire whisk. Cover and freeze about 1 hour or until slushy. Mix well, re-cover, and continue freezing for another 3 hours or until firm.

Each serving equals:

HE: 1 Skim Milk • ½ Fruit • 12 Optional Calories

116 Calories • 0 gm Fat • 8 gm Protein •
21 gm Carbohydrate • 125 mg Sodium •
287 mg Calcium • 0 gm Fiber

DIABETIC: 1 Skim Milk • ½ Fruit

Making Healthy Exchanges Work for You

You're ready now to begin a wonderful journey to better health. In the preceding pages, you've discovered the remarkable variety of good food available to you when you begin eating the Healthy Exchanges way. You've stocked your pantry and learned many of my food preparation "secrets" that will point you on the way to delicious success.

But before I let you go, I'd like to share a few tips that I've learned while traveling toward healthier eating habits. It took me a long time to learn how to eat *smarter*. In fact, I'm still working on it. But I am getting better. For years, I could *inhale* a five-course meal in five minutes flat—and still make room for a second helping of dessert!

Now I follow certain signposts on the road that help me stay on the right path. I hope these ideas will help point you in the right direction as well.

1. **Eat slowly** so your brain has time to catch up with your tummy. Cut and chew each bite slowly. Try putting your fork down between bites. Stop eating as soon as you feel full. Crumple your napkin and throw it on top of your plate so you don't continue to eat when you are no longer hungry.

2. **Smaller plates** may help you feel more satisfied by your food portions *and* limit the amount you can put on the plate.

3. **Watch portion size.** If you are *truly* hungry, you can always add more food to your plate once you've finished your initial serving. But remember to count the additional food accordingly.

4. **Always eat at your dining-room or kitchen table.** You deserve better than nibbling from an open refrigerator or over the sink. Make an attractive place setting, even if you're eating alone. Feed your eyes as well as your stomach. By always eating at a table, you will become much more aware of your true food intake. For some reason, many of us conveniently "forget" the food we swallow while standing over the stove or munching in the car or on the run.

5. **Avoid doing anything else while you are eating.** If you read the paper or watch television while you eat, it's easy to consume too much food without realizing it, because you are concentrating on something else besides what you're eating. Then, when you look down at your plate and see that it's empty, you wonder where all the food went and why you still feel hungry.

Day by day, as you travel the path to good health, it will become easier to make the right choices, to eat *smarter*. But don't ever fool yourself into thinking that you'll be able to put your eating habits on cruise control and forget about them. Making a commitment to eat good healthy food and sticking to it takes some effort. But with all the good-tasting recipes in this Healthy Exchanges cookbook, just think how well you're going to eat—and enjoy it—from now on!

Healthy Lean Bon Appétit!

Recipe Index

I want to hear from you . . .

Besides my family, the love of my life is creating "common folk" healthy recipes and solving everyday cooking questions in *The Healthy Exchanges Way*. Everyone who uses my recipes is considered part of the Healthy Exchanges Family, so please write to me if you have any questions, comments, or suggestions. I will do my best to answer. With your support, I'll continue to stir up even more recipes and cooking tips for the Family in the years to come.

Write to: JoAnna M. Lund
c/o Healthy Exchanges, Inc.
P.O. Box 124
DeWitt, IA 52742

If you prefer, you can fax me at 1-319-659-2126 or contact me via e-mail by writing to HealthyJo@aol.com. (Or visit my Healthy Exchanges Internet web site at: http://www.healthyexchanges.com).

If you're ever in the DeWitt, Iowa, area, stop in and visit me at "The House That Recipes Built" and dine at **JO's Kitchen Cafe**, "Grandma's Comfort Food Made Healthy!"

Ever since I began stirring up Healthy Exchanges recipes, I wanted every dish to be rich in flavor and lively in taste. As part of my pursuit of satisfying eating and healthy living for a lifetime, I decided to create my own line of spices.

JO's Spices are salt-, sugar-, wheat-, and MSG-free, and you can substitute them in any of the recipes calling for traditional spice mixes. If you're interested in hearing more about my special blends, please call Healthy Exchanges at 1-319-659-8234 for more information or to order. If you prefer, write to JO's Spices, c/o Healthy Exchanges, P.O. Box 124, DeWitt, IA 52742.

JO'S SPICES . . . A Healthy Way to Spice Up Your Life™

Now That You've Seen
Grandma's Comfort Food–Made Healthy,
Why Not Order
The Healthy Exchanges Food Newsletter?

If you enjoyed the recipes in this cookbook and would like to cook up even more of these "common folk" healthy dishes, you may want to subscribe to *The Healthy Exchanges Food Newsletter*.

This monthly 12-page newsletter contains 30-plus new recipes *every month* in such columns as:

- Reader Exchange
- Reader Requests
- Recipe Makeover
- Micro Corner
- Dinner for Two

- Crock Pot Luck
- Meatless Main Dishes
- Rise & Shine
- Our Small World

- Brown Bagging It
- Snack Attack
- Side Dishes
- Main Dishes
- Desserts

In addition to all the recipes, other regular features include:

- The Editor's Motivational Corner
- Dining Out Question & Answer
- Cooking Question & Answer
- New Product Alert
- Success Profiles of Winners in the Losing Game
- Exercise Advice from a Cardiac Rehab Specialist
- Nutrition Advice from a Registered Dietitian
- Positive Thought for the Month

Just as in this cookbook, all *Healthy Exchanges Food Newsletter* recipes are calculated in three distinct ways: 1) Weight Loss Choices, 2) Calories with Fat and Fiber Grams, and 3) Diabetic Exchanges.

The cost for a one-year (12-issue) subscription with a special Healthy Exchanges 3-ring binder to store the newsletters in is $28.50, or $22.50 without the binder. To order, simply complete the form and mail to us *or* call our toll-free number and pay with your VISA or MasterCard.

_____ Yes, I want to subscribe to *The Healthy Exchanges Food Newsletter*. $28.50 Yearly Subscription Cost with Storage Binder $_____

$22.50 Yearly Subscription Cost without Binder . . . . $_____

_____ Foreign orders please add $6.00 for money exchange and extra postage. . . . . $_____

_____ I'm not sure, so please send me a sample copy at $2.50. $_____

Please make check payable to HEALTHY EXCHANGES or pay by VISA/MasterCard

CARD NUMBER: _____   EXPIRATION DATE: _____

SIGNATURE: _____

Signature required for all credit card orders.

Or Order Toll-Free, using your credit card, at 1-800-766-8961

NAME: _____

ADDRESS: _____

CITY: _____   STATE: _____   ZIP: _____

TELEPHONE:( )   _____

If additional orders for the newsletter are to be sent to an address other than the one listed above, please use a separate sheet and attach to this form.

MAIL TO: **HEALTHY EXCHANGES**
P.O. BOX 124
DeWitt, IA 52742-0124

1-800-766-8961 for Customer Orders
1-319-659-8234 for Customer Service

Thank you for your order, and for choosing to become a part of the Healthy Exchanges Family!